When FOOTBALL *Was* FOOTBALL

CELTIC

First published in 2010

A catalogue record for this book is available from the British Library

ISBN: 978-0-857330-34-5

Published by Haynes Publishing, Sparkford, Yeovil,
Somerset BA22 7JJ, UK
Tel: 01963 442030 Fax: 01963 440001
Int. tel: +44 1963 442030 Int. fax: +44 1963 440001
E-mail: sales@haynes.co.uk
Website: www.haynes.co.uk

Haynes North America Inc., 861 Lawrence Drive,
Newbury Park, California 91320, USA

All images © Mirrorpix

Creative Director: Kevin Gardner
Designed for Haynes by BrainWave

Printed and bound in the US

When **FOOTBALL** *Was* **FOOTBALL**

CELTIC

A Nostalgic Look at a Century of the Club

Graham McColl

Contents

Foreword

Photographs have a wonderful ability to spark the memory to recall events, and looking at some of the pictures in this book brought back some fantastic memories for me. Seeing a picture of an event that has slipped the mind can let associations flood back and revitalize it all.

For me, these pictures, from the archives of the *Daily Record* and *Daily Mirror*, sharpen my recollections of some great times for Celtic, and not only of the major matches in which the club has participated down the years. Other aspects of being involved with Celtic were also extremely enjoyable, such as participating in the BBC's *Quiz Ball* programme, for which we in the Celtic team enlisted the invaluable help of John Cairney. In tandem with being a fine actor, John has a remarkable range of general knowledge and he helped Jim Craig, Willie Wallace and me to win the tournament several times. They used to fly us all, the Celtic and Rangers players, down from Glasgow to London in a private jet – and memories of such exciting events help encapsulate a truly enjoyable time with the club.

There are some great images of Jock Stein here too, which convey just how passionate he was about the game of football. He wanted players in his team who were entirely committed: he had no time for anyone who was half-hearted in their efforts. That was why his teams were so strong. In some of the pictures of him working with the team that have been reproduced in these pages it is possible to see his dedication to doing all in his power to make Celtic the formidable force that it became under his leadership.

The book also shows magnificent pictures of people such as the great Charlie Tully, who was immensely talented on the field of play and a wonderful character off it. Images of Jimmy Johnstone, of course, bring a smile to the lips of everyone who was fortunate enough to have known the man or seen him play – or, in my case, to have been lucky enough to line up in the same team. Then, in the 1980s, pictures of young players such as Paul McStay, Charlie Nicholas and David Moyes illustrate how the

club was still able to bring in highly talented youngsters at that time. David may not have had quite the same ability as a footballer as Paul and Charlie but he has gone on to become one of the most renowned football managers in British football. I cannot claim that I recognized then that he would go on to do something of that nature, but what I did observe was that he was a very determined boy, keen to make the most of his talents and to become successful. It is interesting to look back and see David as he started out on a fine career in the game.

Other great Celtic players are also featured, such as Jimmy McGrory. He was Celtic manager when I joined the club and I never saw him wearing a tracksuit – always a suit – and he never took training. Alec Boden, who did take the training when I was a young player at Celtic and who is pictured here after the triumphant 1951 Scottish Cup final, was a hardy trainer. We would be getting near the end of a training session and he would shout, "This is the last lap…." So we would hammer into what we thought was our last circuit of the track, and just as we were finishing Alec would shout, "And now this is the second last lap."

The book also shows pictures of my contemporaries, great players with different but strong personalities, such as Ronnie Simpson, Jim Craig, Tommy Gemmell, John Clark, Bobby Murdoch, Willie Wallace, Stevie Chalmers, Bertie Auld, Bobby Lennox and John Hughes. We had a lot of fun in training under Jock, but if any of the boys started messing about you would know all about it. On our visits to Seamill, for example, which are well documented here, we would end up running up and down the beach if something had displeased big Jock.

These are remarkable images and they encapsulate perfectly some wonderful times, terrific people and a magnificent football club.

Billy McNeill

The Greatest Team on Earth
1888-1949

Celtic and Rangers players hover around on the pitch at the end of the 1909 Scottish Cup final replay. After finishing 1-1, the occasion is about to explode into a prolonged riot involving fans of both sides, jointly angry that extra-time, which they had anticipated, is not going to be played after all. No wonder the policemen patrolling the pitch's perimeter look a mite apprehensive. The Cup would subsequently be withheld by the Scottish Football Association for the only time in its history.

> *The rise of the Celtic is the most wonderful of all the club formations that have been disclosed.*
>
> Willie Maley, Celtic manager, 1897–1940

1888 Celtic formed by Brother Walfrid in the East End of Glasgow to raise funds for the Poor Children's Dinner Table charity. 1890 John McLaughlin, representing Celtic, helps drive through the formation of the Scottish League, despite much opposition, and becomes its first secretary. 1892 A 5-1 victory over Queen's Park in a replayed final at Ibrox Park secures Celtic the Scottish Cup, their first national trophy. 1893 Celtic win their first Scottish League title, finishing the season one point ahead of Rangers. 1895 An 11-0 League triumph over Dundee at Celtic Park establishes Celtic's record margin of victory. 1897 Willie Maley is appointed the club's first secretary-manager. 1904 Celtic become the first Scottish club to tour Europe. 1907 The first Scottish League and Cup double is won by Celtic, who finish seven points clear of Dundee in the League and defeat Heart of Midlothian 3-0 in the Cup final. 1909 The Scottish Cup is withheld, and Celtic and Rangers ordered to pay a joint fine of £300 by the SFA after a riot involving both clubs' supporters at the end of the final at Hampden. 1910 A record sixth successive League title goes to Celtic. 1916 Some 106 League goals, a club record, are scored by Celtic in the 1915-16 season. 1925 Alec McNair, aged 41 years and four months, establishes the record for the oldest first-team player to represent Celtic. 1931 John Thomson, the Celtic goalkeeper, tragically dies after sustaining a fractured skull against Rangers. 1937 A record attendance for a European club match, 146,433, is drawn to see Celtic beat Aberdeen 3-1 in the Cup final. 1940 Jimmy McStay replaces Willie Maley as Celtic manager. 1946 Celtic allow Jimmy Delaney, the team's mainstay during the war years, to leave for Manchester United after a dispute over pay.

Jimmy McStay, the Celtic captain, holds up the Scottish Cup after the 1-0 victory over Motherwell in the final at Hampden Park in 1933. Willie Maley (front row, second right), the formidable manager, even produces a smile. Maley was by then in his 37th year as Celtic's secretary-manager. McStay would become his successor in 1940.

Genuine Greatness

The decade that stretched from 1904 to 1914 yielded a series of momentous achievements for Celtic. Willie Maley, the secretary-manager, and the Celtic board of directors had taken a gamble at the turn of the century when they had opted for a policy of nurturing young Scottish players plucked from local clubs rather than the previous approach, whereby the club had paid hefty fees for established and experienced players, often internationals, from all over Britain. It took four trophy-free years for the new practice to start to pay off, but when it did Celtic became almost unstoppable and Maley's methods established the blueprint for how Celtic would go about their business for almost the whole of the 20th century.

RIGHT: The commemorative shield presented to Celtic by the other Scottish League clubs to mark their unprecedented feat of winning six successive Scottish League championship titles between 1904 and 1910.

10

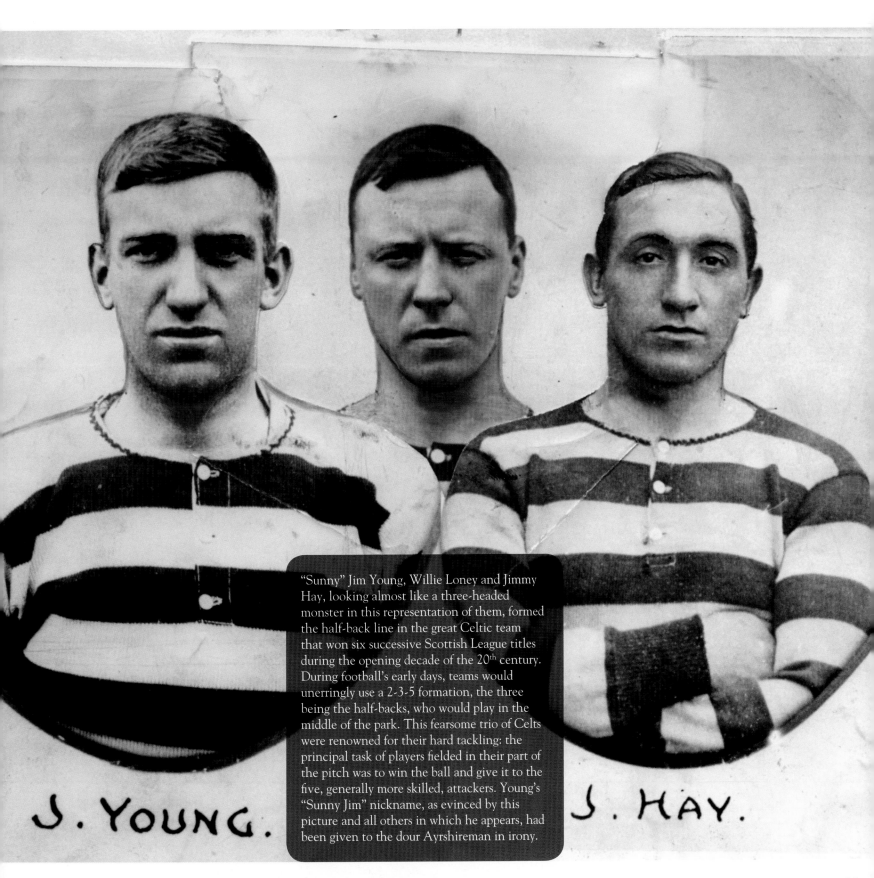

J. YOUNG.

J. HAY.

"Sunny" Jim Young, Willie Loney and Jimmy Hay, looking almost like a three-headed monster in this representation of them, formed the half-back line in the great Celtic team that won six successive Scottish League titles during the opening decade of the 20th century. During football's early days, teams would unerringly use a 2-3-5 formation, the three being the half-backs, who would play in the middle of the park. This fearsome trio of Celts were renowned for their hard tackling: the principal task of players fielded in their part of the pitch was to win the ball and give it to the five, generally more skilled, attackers. Young's "Sunny Jim" nickname, as evinced by this picture and all others in which he appears, had been given to the dour Ayrshireman in irony.

Patsy turns on the style in a match with Heart of Midlothian early in his Celtic career. One opponent can only stand back and admire the Celtic man's trickery.

–LEGENDS– Patsy Gallacher

Patsy Gallacher was one of the first great individualists to capture the imagination of the Celtic support, and he enlivened enormously the dark days of the First World War and early 1920s. At five feet five inches tall and weighing in at just over nine stones, Gallacher had to get the better of opponents almost entirely through verve and delightful deception. "If you put that wee thing on the park you'll get done for manslaughter," Jimmy Quinn, the Celtic centre-forward, told Willie Maley when he first laid eyes on Gallacher; but for all that nimble trickery was the mainstay of Gallacher's game, he was also more than capable of looking after himself.

Patsy's most renowned moment arrived close to the conclusion of his Celtic career, in the Scottish Cup final with Dundee in April 1925, when, with Celtic trailing 1-0, Patsy took possession of the ball inside the Celtic half and went weaving past one opponent after another. Upon reaching the Dundee penalty area and finding the way to goal blocked by hefty defenders he simply clamped the ball between both feet before somersaulting into the net for the most unorthodox of equalizers. A bedazzled Dundee soon succumbed to a second Celtic goal.

> ## The Mighty Atom.
> Nickname for Patsy Gallacher

FOOTBALL –STATS–

Patsy Gallacher

Name: Patrick Gallacher

Born: 1893

Died: 1953

Playing Career: 1911–1932

Clubs: Celtic and Falkirk

Celtic Appearances: 464

Goals: 192

Ireland Appearances: 11

Goals: 0

Irish Free State Appearances: 1

Goals: 0

Daily Record caricatures capture the essence of Malky MacDonald, a doughty centre-half and one of Celtic's most devoted servants during the 1930s, and of Alex Thomson, a rapier-sharp forward who graced the team for 12 years during the 1920s and 1930s. Such drawings, in an era when photography was less widespread than in modern times, were hugely popular in the pages of the newspapers, and nor were they a poor substitute for pictures, as they captured in close detail much of the essence of players and managers at a time when players would rarely be seen up close by the public. As late as the 1950s and 1960s, footballers could walk the streets of Glasgow without being particularly widely recognized, often unnoticed even by their own supporters.

LEFT: Joe Kennaway, the Canadian goalkeeper, on arrival in Glasgow in late 1931, having been brought to Scotland by Celtic as the replacement for John Thomson after the latter had suffered a tragic accident on the field of play in September 1931. Kennaway, when playing for Fall River in the USA, had been the only opposing goalkeeper to have kept a clean sheet against Celtic on their 13-game North American tour in the summer of 1931 and had impressed Willie Maley so much that the Celtic manager, then and there, had compared him to Thomson. A Canadian international, who would also play for Scotland, Kennaway was the first high-profile foreign player to represent Celtic, and he gave the club terrific service for the remainder of the 1930s.

A youngster decides to bypass the turnstiles and join the officially recorded crowd of 118,115 inside Hampden Park at the 1928 Scottish Cup final between Celtic and Rangers. This was the first time Celtic had performed in front of a six-figure attendance at a final – less happily, the match ended in a 4-0 defeat.

John Thomson stretches to gather the ball during the 1928 Scottish Cup final with Rangers.

The Prince of Goalkeepers

The 1920s proved a testing decade for Celtic, with Rangers dominating Scottish football for the first time but new, young recruits John Thomson (below left) and Willie McGonagle (below right), here with Eddie McGarvie, the trainer, were among the players who gave Celtic much hope for the following decade. Both players made their debuts in 1927 and showed huge promise. Tragically, Thomson would lose his life in September 1931, when, during a match with Rangers at Ibrox, he dived at the feet of Sam English, the Rangers centre-forward, and, fatally, suffered a depressed fracture of the skull in the resultant collision.

Thomson, 22 at the time of his death, had already established himself as Scotland's first-choice international goalkeeper. He had been prominent in the Celtic team that beat Motherwell 4-2 in the replayed Scottish Cup final of April 1931, which had seen the Celts lift their first national trophy in four years. Herbert Chapman, the Arsenal manager, had described him as the best goalkeeper in the world and had been keen on signing him. McGonagle, an all-action, wholehearted full-back, would conclude his Celtic career more happily in the mid-1930s, having made 325 appearances for the club.

John Thomson, under pressure, turns a scoring attempt over the crossbar during the 1931 Scottish Cup final with Motherwell.

Anxious players of both sides look on as John Thomson is carried off the pitch at Ibrox.

SUNDAY MAIL

BRIGHTEST BEST

MORNING SPECIAL

No 1198   SUNDAY, SEPTEMBER 6, 1931   PRICE TWOPENCE

CELTIC GOALKEEPER'S DEATH

NEW MOVES IN NATIONAL CRISIS.

T.U.C. TO REVEAL VITAL SECRETS.

DRAMA OF LAST MEETING WITH LABOUR CABINET TO BE DISCLOSED.

SOCIALIST SPLIT RUMOURS.

CUSTODIAN'S TRAGIC JOURNEY.

TRAGEDY MARS CLASH OF FOOTBALL GIANTS.

CELTIC'S BRILLIANT KEEPER DIES FROM INJURIES.

PARENTS' DASH TO BEDSIDE.

Mourners at John Thomson's funeral take his coffin from the window of the family home in Fife, on 9th September 1931, four days after his untimely death.

RIGHT: John Thomson's mother (second left) on the day of her son's funeral at Bowhill Cemetery, is accompanied by her daughters and by Mrs Sam English (second right), the wife of the Rangers player. No blame was attached to English for Thomson's death.

17

The Scottish Cup 1937

When the tickets for the final of the 1937 Scottish Cup were put on sale, supporters of Aberdeen and Celtic found that they were slightly more expensive than had been expected, ranging from one shilling for the Hampden Park terraces to 10 shillings and sixpence for the stand. This did nothing to deter the enthusiasm of both sets of supporters: in fact the 146,433 who crammed into the ground on 24th April that year created the European record attendance for a match between club sides – one that remains unbroken.

Celtic were at the time re-emerging as a powerful force in Scottish football. They had won the League the previous year for the first time in a decade while Aberdeen had concluded the 1936-7 season as runners-up to Rangers, causing enthusiastic hordes of supporters to travel down from the north-east to see the Pittodrie side participate in their first Scottish Cup final. An estimated 20,000 supporters were locked out of the ground and had to listen to the roars inside to try to follow a dramatic encounter that saw Celtic emerge as 2-1 victors.

ABOVE: Chic Geatons, the distinguished right-half, who spent 14 years with Celtic, crosses from the right wing during the 1937 final, challenged by Willie Mills, the Aberdeen forward.

ABOVE: A happy band of Celts celebrate in front of the now deserted, litter-strewn terraces after the 1937 Scottish Cup final. Willie Buchan (second left) and Johnny Crum (second right), Celtic's goalscorers in the final, clutch the Cup, while Willie Maley (far left), the manager, celebrates another trophy 40 years after his appointment as Celtic's secretary-manager. Jimmy Quinn, the first great Celtic centre-forward, and star of the six-in-a row 1904-10 team, is in the centre, while Jimmy McMenemy, his former team-mate and by 1937 an influential trainer at Celtic, is on the right.

–LEGENDS– Jimmy McGrory

Two accolades attach themselves strongly to Jimmy McGrory. He is, firstly, and indisputably, the greatest goalscorer in Celtic's history. Secondly, and more by way of reputation than statistic, he is described unerringly by all who encountered him as the nicest man they ever met. McGrory achieved the rare feat for a centre-forward of scoring a greater number of goals than the amount of games he played – an achievement all the more noteworthy in that he turned out for Celtic in over 400 League and Cup matches between the mid-1920s and the late 1930s.

His powerful build helped him to thrive in the brawny, physically demanding game of the interwar years, when heavy footballs and heavy boots were in use and his 50 first division goals in the 1935-6 season, when he was enjoying an Indian summer to his career, remain the record for Scotland's top flight. Against Dunfermline Athletic in January 1928, he hit a hat-trick in the opening nine minutes and went on to score another five as Celtic won 9-0. That tally of eight in a single match remains the individual scoring record for Scotland's top division and helps underline why McGrory remains peerless in the story of Celtic and of Scottish football.

FOOTBALL –STATS–

Jimmy McGrory

Name: James Edward McGrory

Born: 1904

Died: 1982

Playing Career: 1921–1937

Clubs: Celtic

Celtic Appearances: 445

Goals: 468

Scotland Appearances: 7

Goals: 6

> " A Celtic fan cried in a pause
> While Parkhead's fog hung hoary
> We dinna need yer Santa Claus
> While we ha'e Jimmy McGrory.
>
> Poem in the *Sunday Mail* after Jimmy McGrory had
> scored a hat-trick against Aberdeen at Christmas 1935 "

Jimmy McGrory in action against Motherwell in the 1930s; foul means appear to be being employed here to prevent McGrory getting yet another goal.

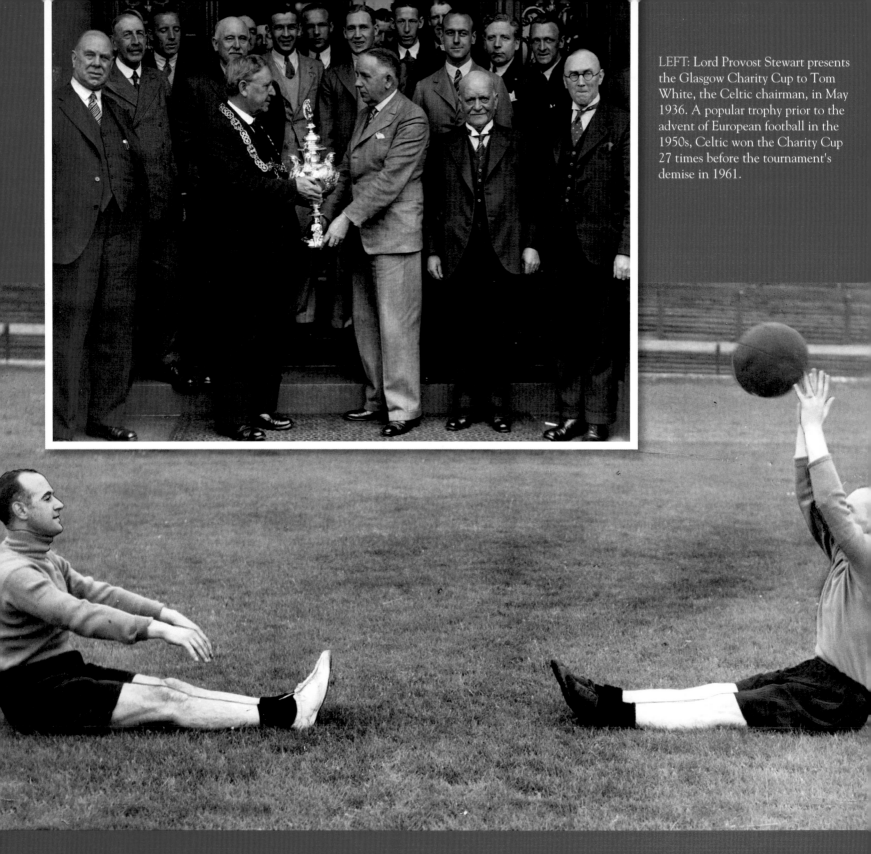

LEFT: Lord Provost Stewart presents the Glasgow Charity Cup to Tom White, the Celtic chairman, in May 1936. A popular trophy prior to the advent of European football in the 1950s, Celtic won the Charity Cup 27 times before the tournament's demise in 1961.

The Second World War is on the horizon but at Celtic Park in the summer of 1939 it is business as usual as Willie Lyon, the centre-half, (left), and Chic Geatons, the right-half, get down to some serious pre-season work with the medicine ball.

–LEGENDS– Jimmy Delaney

Jimmy Delaney was a pivotal force in Celtic's spirited and exciting revival during the second half of the 1930s. He was a winger but not of the traditional type who would aim only to hit the goal-line and sling over a cross for the centre-forward. Jimmy, instead, might just as easily drive inside with the ball and find a team-mate with a direct and devastating pass or, if it was on, have a shot at goal himself. Equally, he could still go wide in the traditional fashion and cross, hard and fast, the way goalkeepers do not like it. His flexibility made him an enormous asset to a Celtic team whose players, in the late 1930s, had begun to experiment with positioning and tactics.

An utterly dedicated professional, Jimmy would train assiduously and then do a bit extra by carrying out his own exercises. A severe arm injury, which he suffered in a League match with Arbroath in 1939, kept him out of action for two years but, when he returned to fitness, he carried the Celtic team during the war years. This counted for little, though, with the directors who baulked at his demand for a post-war pay rise, and he was transferred to Manchester United in 1946. There his talents would be central to the success of Matt Busby's first great United team.

FOOTBALL –STATS–

Jimmy Delaney

Name: James Delaney

Born: 1914 Died: 1989

Playing Career: 1934–1957

Clubs: Celtic, Manchester United, Aberdeen, Falkirk, Derry City, Cork Athletic, Elgin City

Celtic Appearances: 160 (not including wartime)

Goals: 74

Scotland Appearances: 13 (not including wartime)

Goals: 3

ABOVE: The Scottish Cup winner's medal awarded to Jimmy Delaney after Celtic's victory over Aberdeen in the 1937 final.

LEFT: Jimmy Delaney looks to manoeuvre the ball past an opponent in a match with Partick Thistle at Firhill in January 1946.

"

He was one of the greatest wingers the game of football has ever seen.

Johnny Paton, team-mate, on Jimmy Delaney

"

23

Going Nowhere Fast

Celtic emerged from the Second World War with Jimmy McGrory in place as their new manager, but the post-war years proved difficult for the club. They even came close to relegation near the end of the 1947-8 season; the only time in Celtic's history that they have faced the serious possibility of demotion from the top flight. Celtic travelled to Dundee in their final League fixture. They needed a win to be sure of safety, and, in front of 31,000 at Dens Park, came from 2-1 down to win 3-2, with two late goals from Jock Weir sealing the winger's hat-trick.

"There is no question that the feeling among the players was that if we didn't win that match we would have gone down," claimed Johnny Paton, the left-winger at Dundee that day. Jock Weir, a dapper ladies' man, would buy a new suit every month, a huge extravagance in the post-war years, and he was "the life and soul of the party", according to Paton. Jimmy Hogan, a coach with a remarkable pedigree, was appointed in the summer of 1948 to improve standards at the club after the scare of relegation, but although some players proved receptive to him, others resisted the idea of specialist coaching, and the club's malaise would continue for some years.

Willie Miller, the Celtic goalkeeper, (left), Jock Weir, the outside-right, (centre) and Johnny Paton, the outside-left, lap the track at Celtic Park to get into shape in the summer of 1948, relieved to be playing top-flight football again, while a member of the ground staff carries out his own preparations for the new season.

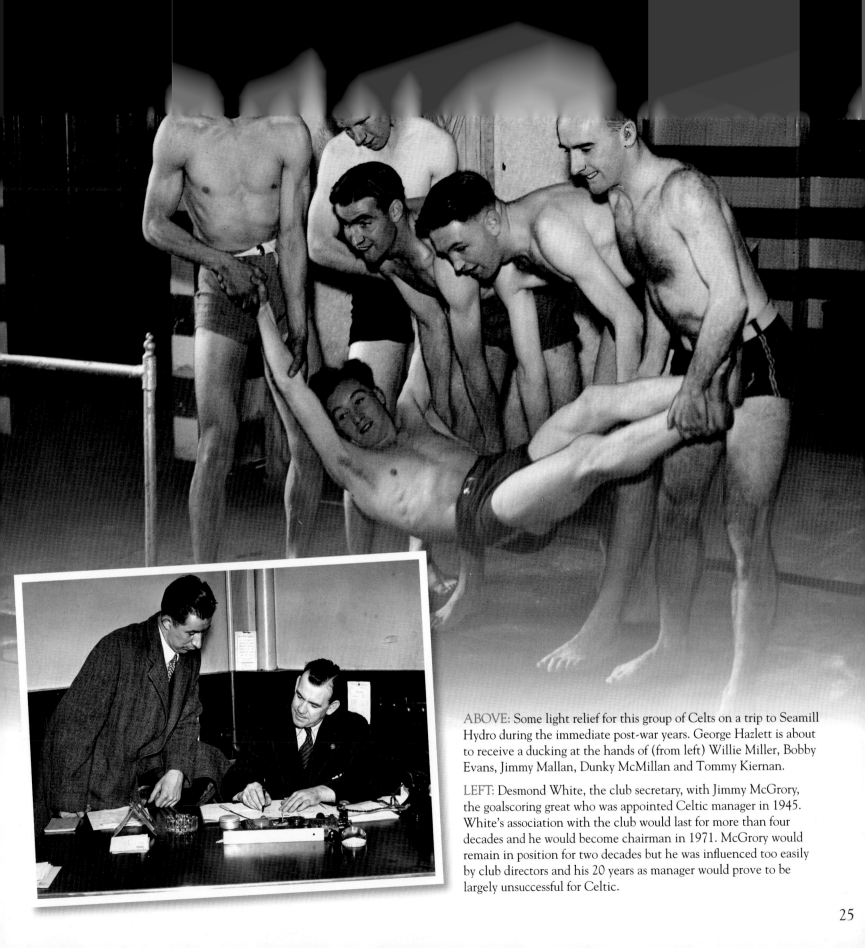

ABOVE: Some light relief for this group of Celts on a trip to Seamill Hydro during the immediate post-war years. George Hazlett is about to receive a ducking at the hands of (from left) Willie Miller, Bobby Evans, Jimmy Mallan, Dunky McMillan and Tommy Kiernan.

LEFT: Desmond White, the club secretary, with Jimmy McGrory, the goalscoring great who was appointed Celtic manager in 1945. White's association with the club would last for more than four decades and he would become chairman in 1971. McGrory would remain in position for two decades but he was influenced too easily by club directors and his 20 years as manager would prove to be largely unsuccessful for Celtic.

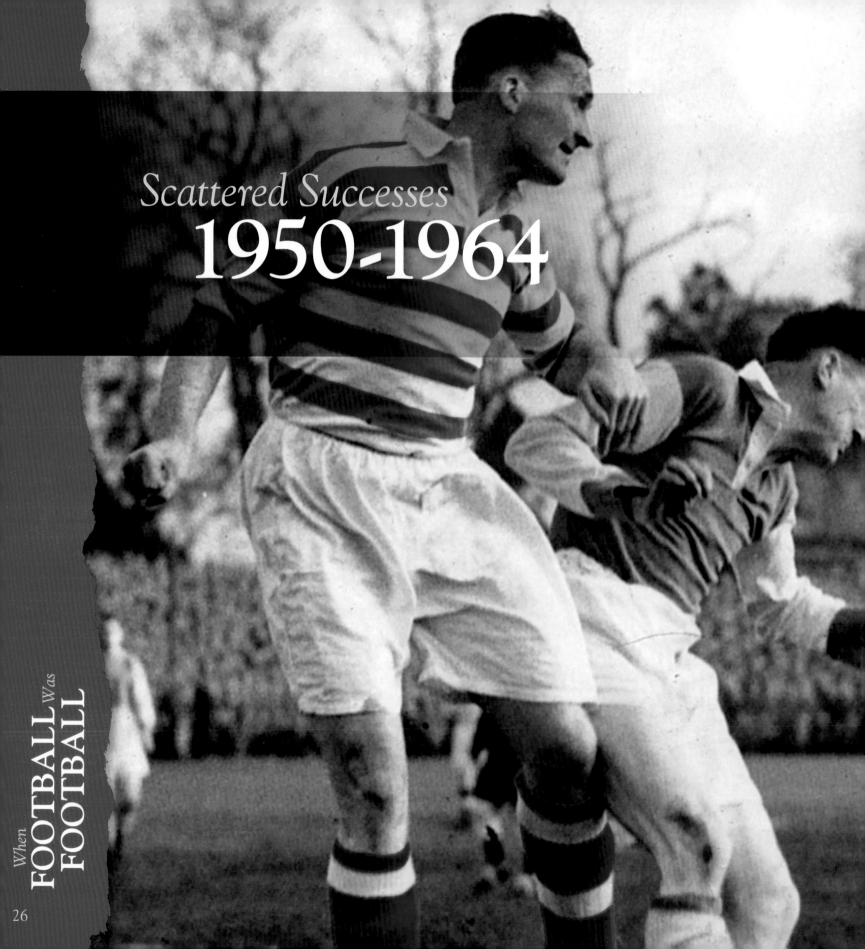

Scattered Successes

1950-1964

Jock Stein winning a header in a match with Stirling Albion in 1955.

1951 Celtic beat Motherwell 1-0 in the Scottish Cup final to win a national competition for the first time in 13 years. Jock Stein is brought to Celtic from Llanelli, the Welsh club, as a back-up centre-half. **1953** Arsenal, Manchester United and Hibernian fall to Celtic as they win the Coronation Cup, an eight-team tournament held in honour of Queen Elizabeth II's accession to the throne. **1954** Captained by the influential Jock Stein, Celtic win the Scottish Cup and League double for the first time since 1914. **1956** Celtic win the League Cup for the first time, defeating Partick Thistle 3-0 in the replayed final. **1957** A 7-1 victory over Rangers wins Celtic their second successive League Cup and establishes the record margin of victory for a Scottish or English Cup final. **1959** Floodlight pylons are erected at Celtic Park. **1962** A Fairs Cup tie with Valencia, the holders, sees Celtic make their debut in European competition. **1963** Jimmy Johnstone makes his Celtic debut in a 6-0 defeat at Kilmarnock. **1964** Celtic reach the semi-finals of the European Cup Winners' Cup but throw away a 3-0 first-leg lead over MTK Budapest to lose 4-3 on aggregate.

Celtic with the Coronation Cup they won in 1953, one of only a few 1950s successes for the club. Jock Stein, the team captain, is third from left in the front row. Neilly Mochan and Jimmy Walsh, scorers in the 2-0 win over Hibernian in the final, flank him right and left respectively.

Post-war Struggles

When Celtic met Motherwell in the 1951 Scottish Cup final, 13 years had passed since the club had won a national trophy, so the Celtic supporters in the 132,000 crowd were desperate for a glimmer of success. It proved to be an undistinguished match, with just the one goal, scored by John McPhail, the Celtic centre-forward. With 12 minutes gone, McPhail eased between two defenders, let the ball bounce once and then sent a dipping shot over John Johnstone in the Motherwell goal. That special moment, when McPhail broke through to end Celtic's longest-ever trophy drought, imprinted itself firmly on the minds of a generation of Celtic supporters.

RIGHT: John McPhail holds aloft the Scottish Cup after the 1951 final, chaired by Alec Boden, the uncompromising centre-half, and Sean Fallon, the full-back.

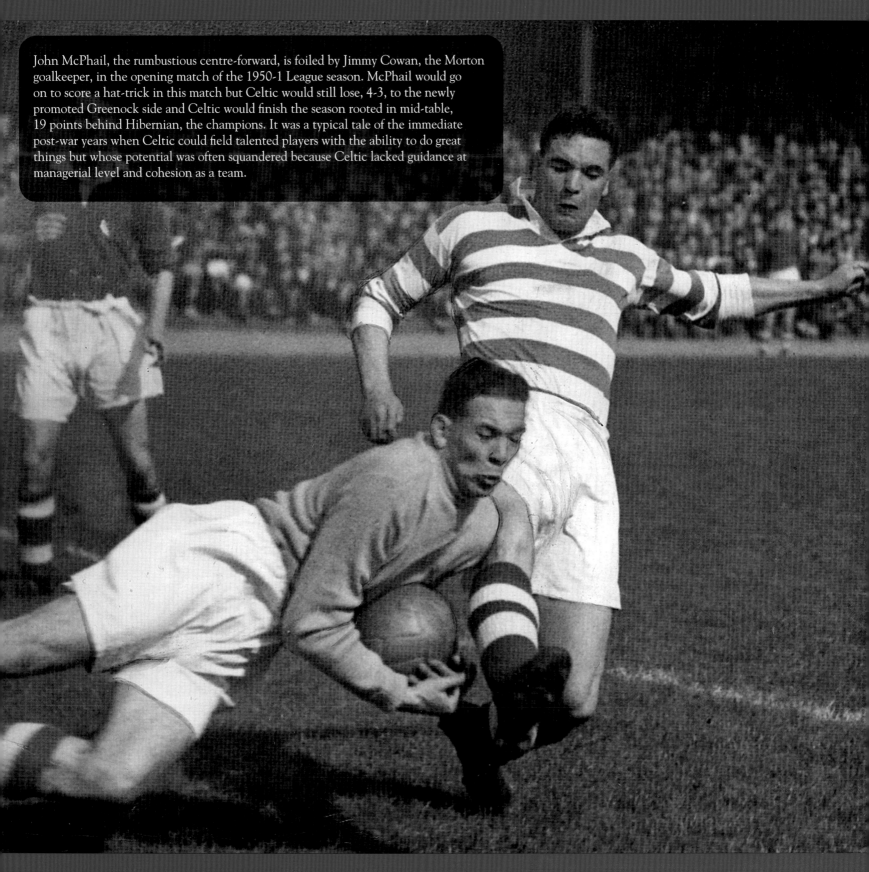

John McPhail, the rumbustious centre-forward, is foiled by Jimmy Cowan, the Morton goalkeeper, in the opening match of the 1950-1 League season. McPhail would go on to score a hat-trick in this match but Celtic would still lose, 4-3, to the newly promoted Greenock side and Celtic would finish the season rooted in mid-table, 19 points behind Hibernian, the champions. It was a typical tale of the immediate post-war years when Celtic could field talented players with the ability to do great things but whose potential was often squandered because Celtic lacked guidance at managerial level and cohesion as a team.

Going Places

Jimmy Thomson, the Hibernian centre-forward, heads for goal against Celtic in a League match in front of 45,000 at Easter Road in April 1954. He failed to hit the target and Celtic went on to win 3-0 in this, the penultimate game of their first championship-winning season for 16 years – the lengthiest stretch between titles that the club has ever endured. Unusually for a Celtic team, this was one with its greatest strength in defence as epitomized by Jock Stein (left) and Bobby Evans (right) the players most closely watching Thomson.

LEFT: Celtic players enjoy a pre-match meal at Ferrari's restaurant on Buchanan Street, Glasgow, before travelling through to Edinburgh for the League match with Hibernian in April 1954. This Italian establishment was the regular venue at which the players would assemble before matches.

BELOW: A group of Celts on the boat deck as they prepare to sail for Ireland and a three-match tour in May 1955. Jimmy Gribben (far left), a member of the training staff, was the man who had suggested that Jock Stein (fourth from left), should be recruited from Llanelli as a back-up centre-half in 1951. It had been expected within the club that Stein might never play a first-team game. Instead, injuries gave him an immediate opportunity to make his debut and he never looked back from that point, becoming the on-field organizer who inspired the 1953-4 League and Cup double.

The smartly turned-out Celtic team of the mid-1950s prepare to take the train to Aberdeen – on arrival in the Granite City, the players would habitually walk from the railway station to Pittodrie to stretch their legs after the long rail trip. This well-presented bunch are, from left: Jimmy Walsh, Bobby Evans, Charlie Tully, John Higgins, Johnny Bonnar, Jock Stein, Mike Haughney, Willie Fernie, Alec Boden, Bertie Peacock and Sean Fallon.

–LEGENDS–

Charlie Tully

Charlie Tully was an audacious Irish inside-forward who joined Celtic in the summer of 1948, just as the club was needing a boost, following a season in which they had almost been relegated. Cheeky Charlie, whose array of skills was matched only by his devilment on and off the pitch, soon became the subject of a personality cult among the club's supporters. Among his repertoire of audacious tricks was sitting on the ball and using a throw-in to deflect the ball off an unsuspecting opponent's back to win a corner kick.

The most noteworthy of Tully's exploits came in a Scottish Cup third-round tie at Falkirk in February 1953, when he took a corner and sent the ball directly into the net. The referee insisted that the kick be retaken because he believed that the ball would have had to have been improperly positioned, outside the arc. Tully simply sent the ball directly into the net once again. His unpredictable skills in the inside-forward position were key to the Coronation Cup victory of 1953, the Scottish League and Cup double of 1953-4 and Celtic's first League Cup final triumphs, in 1956 and 1957, the latter being the 7-1 rout of Rangers.

FOOTBALL –STATS–

Charlie Tully

Name: Charles Patrick Tully

Born: 1924

Died: 1971

Playing Career: 1942–1959

Clubs: Belfast Celtic and Celtic

Celtic Appearances: 319

Goals: 43

Northern Ireland Appearances: 10

Goals: 3

> *He was a one-off character. I've never met anybody like him.*
>
> Jimmy Walsh, Celtic player of the 1950s, on Charlie Tully

Charlie Tully's carefree approach to life added some extra swing to Celtic during the 1950s. The team-mates who, along with their stylish companions, are enjoying his playground antics here are (from left to right) Sean Fallon, Mike Haughney, Bertie Peacock and John McPhail.

Charlie gets down to some not-so-serious reading with John McPhail (centre), his closest friend at Celtic, and George Young, captain of Rangers and Scotland.

A Fitting Finale

RIGHT: The result of the 1957 League Cup final – Celtic 7 Rangers 1 – remains the record scoreline in any national Cup final in England and Scotland. Charlie Tully, when asked afterwards what the time was, replied "Seven past Niven" in reference to George, the Rangers goalkeeper. For the group of players, including Tully and Bertie Peacock, who had been stalwarts of the Celtic team throughout the 1950s, and who were now coming to the end of their years of service, this was a fitting final reward.

Peacock and Tully with the League Cup

Billy McPhail scores his third and Celtic's sixth goal in the 7-1 demolition of Rangers in October 1957.

Billy McPhail and Bobby Collins, two of the heroes of the 7-1 victory over Rangers, with the League Cup. Celtic had first won the trophy in 1956 with McPhail scoring twice and Collins once in the 3-0 victory over Partick Thistle, a replay, after the first match had been drawn 0-0.

LEFT: Mike Jackson, the 18-year-old Celtic winger, challenges Bill Brown, the Dundee goalkeeper, in a 0-0 draw at Celtic Park in December 1957. Only two months had passed since Celtic's 7-1 victory over Rangers in the League Cup final but it was clear even to the staid management inside Celtic that the team needed an infusion of youngsters. Players such as Jackson would receive their coaching at first-team level less from the training staff at Celtic than from the more experienced professionals who played alongside them.

Fun Times

ABOVE: Bobby Evans, a player vital to Celtic during the 1950s, in fun mode at Ferrari's restaurant in 1957. Bertie Peacock, in the background, has more serious matters in mind, as does Bobby Collins, right.

LEFT: Billy McPhail, the Celtic centre-forward whose goals were vital to the team of the late 1950s, with Fifi, his wife, at a theatrical ball.

A thumbs-up shows a degree of contentment on the part of Billy McNeill as he, Bertie Auld (left), Pat Crerand (second left) and John Divers listen to the Scottish Cup draw on the radio in February 1961. These players were among a number who represented the new, youthful face of Celtic at the start of the decade and they had all been in the Celtic team that had beaten Falkirk 3-1 in the opening round of the Cup, in January. The draw would prove kind to them in February, presenting them with ties that month at home to Montrose and away to Raith Rovers, which they would win comfortably, 6-0 and 4-1 respectively.

The group of young Celtic players of which Auld, McNeill, Crerand and Divers were part was described as the Kelly Kids, a nickname that echoed Matt Busby's great Busby Babes – but there the similarities ended. At Old Trafford, the Babes were guided by one of the great Scottish managers and by Jimmy Murphy, a dedicated coach. Celtic's version lacked the same type of organization and know-how and, as the name suggested, was under the control of Robert Kelly, the chairman, who lacked the dedicated football knowledge to make the scheme work properly. Auld, a refined player but with a temper that the chairman disliked, was allowed to leave by Kelly for Birmingham City at the end of this 1960-1 season, which would also conclude with defeat in the Scottish Cup final to Dunfermline Athletic, who had recruited Jock Stein as manager from his position as Celtic reserve-team coach in early 1960.

Cup Chaos

Crowd disturbances are not an entirely modern phenomenon – at Celtic's Scottish Cup semi-final with St Mirren in March 1962, played at Ibrox Park, fans spilled on to the pitch as Celtic turned in a poor performance and were outplayed in losing 3-1. Willie Fernie, who had been prominent in Celtic teams of the 1950s but who had been transferred to St Mirren in late 1961, scored the opening goal for the Paisley side in a match watched by close to 60,000 spectators, and with little more than half an hour gone, St Mirren, who were struggling to avoid relegation that season, had streaked into a 3-0 lead.

After John Hughes, the Celtic centre-forward, had a second-half goal disallowed, hundreds of spectators poured on to the pitch from both ends of the ground, stopping the match for quarter of an hour, and it required the intervention of mounted police to help restore calm. An amusing aspect of a largely serious outbreak of disorder, in which punch-ups were broken up by the police, arrived when young Celtic supporters, having rushed on to the pitch, surrounded Frank Haffey, the goalkeeper, to ask him to sign their autograph books, only to be given short shrift by him and ordered to return whence they came.

Dunky MacKay and Tommy Gemmell, the Celtic full-backs, combine to clear the ball during a League Cup match with Rangers at Ibrox in August 1963; with goalkeeper Frank Haffey grounded. For Celtic, this was a painful period of Rangers domination and in the 1963-4 season, Celtic lost not only this match 3-0 but all five League and Cup encounters with their great rivals.

Dunky MacKay, the Celtic full-back, clears the ball during the 1963 Scottish Cup final. Teeming crowds routinely formed the backdrop to major events such as these during the first half of the 1960s – this replayed final drew more than 250,000 spectators to the two matches at Hampden Park. The more routine matches for Celtic saw attendances at Celtic Park drop alarmingly as a young team, with no real leadership or guidance, failed to click. It was Robert Kelly, the chairman, who was the dominant force off the field, rather than Jimmy McGrory, the manager, with Kelly effectively picking the team.

During the late 1950s, Jock Stein, having been forced to retire through injury, was appointed reserve-team coach and did a marvellous job with the young players at his disposal before leaving for Dunfermline Athletic in 1960. His departure was felt keenly by those who had been under his guidance, such as MacKay, a fine, athletic right-back. Celtic drew 1-1 with Rangers in the initial 90 minutes yet failed to settle the 1963 final; after Kelly, on a whim, had

Celtic Park as it looked in the mid-1960s, from the east terracing, with the press box on top of the roof of the stand, as at Hampden. Designed by Glasgow architects Duncan & Kerr and built in 1929, this stand had room for just 4,800 seats, with the rest of the ground consisting entirely of terraces that could hold up to 80,000 people. Expanses of grass stretched behind each goal, making spectating difficult from either end of the ground, but large enough for players to use for five-a-side matches in training.

Into Europe

Jim Kennedy, Pat Crerand, Mike Jackson, Billy Price, Billy McNeill and Frank Haffey acknowledge the crowd on a lap of honour, a rarity in the football of the early 1960s, after a 3-1 defeat to Real Madrid. This friendly match at Celtic Park, on 10th September 1962, was even more highly anticipated than Celtic's official debut in European competition, against Valencia, in the Fairs Cup, later that month. A 76,000 all-ticket crowd watched the Real match and although Celtic lost, the players gave a good account of themselves, inducing the demand for them to reappear after the match. There were 30,000 fewer at Celtic Park to see Celtic attempt to retrieve a 4-2 first-leg defeat to Valencia in the second leg of the Fairs Cup tie in late October 1962, a match that ended 2-2.

The Celtic players applaud Real Madrid as they leave the Celtic Park pitch. At the time, Real were indisputably the world's most illustrious and glamorous club. Led by Alfredo di Stefano, the Argentinian (sixth from right), Real had appeared in seven of the eight European Cup finals to date, winning six of them. With Celtic struggling badly at the time, Real's visit was almost like that of a team from another planet. The three nearest Celtic players are, from left, Pat Crerand, Bobby Murdoch and Mike Jackson.

ABOVE: Jimmy Johnstone, Bobby Lennox and Charlie Gallagher are escorted to their plane by an air stewardess at Renfrew Airport prior to departure for the first leg of Celtic's Fairs Cup tie with Barcelona in November 1964.

BELOW: John Cushley (left) and Hugh Maxwell swot up on a tourist guide to Barcelona before flying out to Spain for the 1964 Fairs Cup tie. Maxwell, a forward, had just signed from Falkirk but would remain at Celtic for only seven months before becoming one of the first players to depart under the new management of Jock Stein, who sold him on to St Johnstone in June 1965.

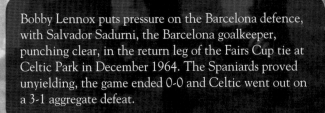

Bobby Lennox puts pressure on the Barcelona defence, with Salvador Sadurni, the Barcelona goalkeeper, punching clear, in the return leg of the Fairs Cup tie at Celtic Park in December 1964. The Spaniards proved unyielding, the game ended 0-0 and Celtic went out on a 3-1 aggregate defeat.

51

Working Men

Training, early 1960s-style, as Frank Haffey, the goalkeeper, skips his way to fitness on the running track at Celtic Park, with Jim Kennedy (left) and Billy Price swinging the rope.

Some shooting practice for five young Celts in February 1964 under the scrutiny of Neilly Mochan, following his appointment as a coach at the club. Mochan would remain a trusted member of the backroom staff until the 1990s. Here he watches (from left) Bobby Murdoch, Charlie Gallagher, Frank Brogan, Paddy Turner and Stevie Chalmers get their shots away.

Pat Crerand and Charlie Gallagher, cousins and Celtic team-mates, enjoy a kickabout in their native Gorbals in 1960, with one youngster much more interested in the photographer than in the ball.

LEFT: Mrs Kelly, the wife of the Celtic chairman, assisted by James Farrell, a director of the club from the 1960s until the 1990s, makes the first half-time draw at Celtic Park, in 1964.

RIGHT: Seeing a dog on the pitch used to afford an interval of light relief for football fans everywhere and Celtic Park was no exception. Here, during a match in the early 1960s, Pat Crerand attempts to persuade the latest canine invader to leave the field of play by hurling its collar in the direction of the sidelines.

Pat Crerand waves from the window of his Gorbals home. He would wave a final farewell to Celtic after being transferred to Manchester United for £56,000 in February 1963.

1965-1967

"
We don't want to be compared to the legends of the past. We want to create our own legends.

Jock Stein in 1966
"

John Hughes powers through to score Celtic's second goal in their 5-3 victory over Dundee in the 1967 League Cup final.

The achievements of the Lisbon Lions were unprecedented in British football and nor will they ever be matched. Not only did they become the first British club to reach the European Cup final but they won it. Not only did they win it but they defeated Internazionale of Milan, the world's richest football club, to do so and with a team drawn, famously, not only exclusively from within Scotland but from within 30 miles of Glasgow. They also became the first team from northern Europe to win a tournament that, until then, had belonged exclusively to the tactical sophisticates of southern Europe, while Celtic won the trophy with a team from the Scottish League, then, as now, regarded as hugely inferior in standard by many outside of Scotland. In addition to all that, Celtic won the final in Lisbon by playing glorious attacking football, making theirs the perfect victory. There are many elsewhere in Britain who feel that their club should have been first to win the European Cup – notably the followers of Liverpool and Manchester United – and that only misfortune had prevented them doing so. The difference between them and that Celtic team was that where those others got close to the final, Celtic held their nerve to win the European Cup and make the breakthrough.

Jock Stein had arrived at Celtic as manager in March 1965 to find a club moribund after eight years without winning a national trophy. Players such as Billy McNeill were considering offers to leave while others, such as Jimmy Johnstone, Bobby Murdoch and Tommy Gemmell, who would become essential to Stein, had had their style cramped by the shortcomings of the previous management. Stein's greatest act was to free such players and, through employing his exceptional powers of motivation combined with discipline, to make every man in his team play both with creativity and also within the tight framework that he created for them. It brought Celtic a period rich both in style and success.

Delight at being at the dawn of an exciting era of success for Celtic is evident on the faces of Billy McNeill and John Hughes as they parade the newly won League Cup after beating Rangers in October 1965.

You put your right leg out… Billy McNeill leads Stevie Chalmers, Bobby Murdoch and Joe McBride in training for their Scottish Cup semi-final with Dunfermline Athletic in the spring of 1966. Jock Stein insisted upon his players working hard in training and demanded to see utter commitment and concentration from them in every session. For all the emphasis on hard work, though, one of the things his players appreciated greatly was his introduction of much more ballwork in training, something that had been badly overlooked prior to his arrival as manager.

Getting Down to Business

Jock Stein loved training, being in the thick of things and joining in with the players. Here, John Hughes manages to elude him with the ball.

–LEGENDS–

Bobby Murdoch

Bobby Murdoch was among the major beneficiaries of the arrival of Jock Stein at Celtic Park in early 1965. Until that point he had been deployed as an inside-forward, but had been struggling to stay with the play up front. Stein switched the heavily-built Murdoch to midfield, which allowed him to display his previously well-disguised talent for passing the ball with magnificent accuracy. He also packed a tremendous shot, which he could use to full effect by latching on to the ball when powering through from midfield to within shooting range of goal.

It was appropriate that it was from a Murdoch cross that Stevie Chalmers scored Celtic's winning goal in the European Cup final in Lisbon because Murdoch and Bertie Auld, his midfield partner, had put in perfect performances on the day. Another Murdoch goal, in the 1970 European Cup semi-final with Leeds United, secured Celtic's place in that final. Bobby Murdoch's exceptional ability to push and pull a match in whichever direction he chose meant that when he was at his best, Celtic purred along as smoothly as a Rolls-Royce.

FOOTBALL –STATS–

Bobby Murdoch

Name: Robert Murdoch

Born: 1944

Died: 2001

Playing Career: 1959–1976

Clubs: Celtic and Middlesbrough

Celtic Appearances: 484

Goals: 102

Scotland Appearances: 12

Goals: 5

Bobby Murdoch settles down to enjoy some sweet 1960s sounds from his long-playing records in December 1963.

> *The finest player in Britain.*
>
> Jock Stein on Bobby Murdoch

ABOVE: Bobby Murdoch forms a bulwark between Ronnie Simpson, his goalkeeper, and the Rangers attack, during the rainswept and decisive match at Ibrox in May 1967 that concluded in a 2-2 draw and gave Celtic their second successive title.

RIGHT: Bobby, at home with Kathleen, his wife, passes on some tips to Robert, his son.

ABOVE: Ayrton Inacio, one of four Brazilians
brought to Celtic on trial during the summer of 1965,
shoots and scores in a match between the reserve
sides of Celtic and Motherwell, which drew a crowd
of 11,000 to Celtic Park, attracted largely by the
prospect of seeing Inacio and his fellow Brazilians. It
was a revolutionary move for Jock Stein to consider
bringing in players from South America at a time
when foreign players were rare in the British game but
after an extensive trial period the manager decided
not to sign any of the Brazilian players after failing to
agree contractual terms with their agent.

RIGHT: Jock Stein's standing in Scottish football
was so high in 1965 that shortly after he had become
Celtic manager, he was also appointed manager of the
Scotland national team on a part-time basis. Here, in
that capacity, he greets Pat Crerand, the former Celt,
prior to a visit to Poland for a World Cup tie, with
Billy McNeill also in attendance.

John "Yogi Bear" Hughes steps up to score his and Celtic's second penalty of the 1965 League Cup final, which would conclude in a 2-1 victory for Celtic, a win that Jock Stein regarded as utterly vital to the club. During the first half of the 1960s, Celtic had had a poor record against Rangers and although Celtic had still managed to reach Cup finals, they had always lost out on the big day. Now, in 1965, Celtic had won both of the Cup finals held in that year – Stein's team had won the Scottish Cup in the spring against Dunfermline Athletic – and in the second had shown that they could defeat Rangers when it really mattered.

FAR LEFT: Jimmy Johnstone walks out with Agnes, his fiancée, in their native Viewpark.

ABOVE: Billy McNeill, with wife, Liz.

LEFT: Kathryn and Bobby Lennox prepare to cut the cake at their wedding in June 1967, with Charlie Gallagher, Willie O'Neill and Jock Stein in close attendance.

During the Jock Stein years at Celtic, as the demand to see his great teams grew, long and snaking queues outside the ground would become a common sight. Here supporters wait patiently for the chance to buy tickets for the first leg of the European Cup Winners' Cup semi-final with Liverpool in the spring of 1966. The English club were the champions elect in their country and drew an all-ticket crowd of 80,000 to Celtic Park for a match that Celtic dominated entirely, with the 1-0 scoreline a poor reflection of the number of chances Stein's team had created.

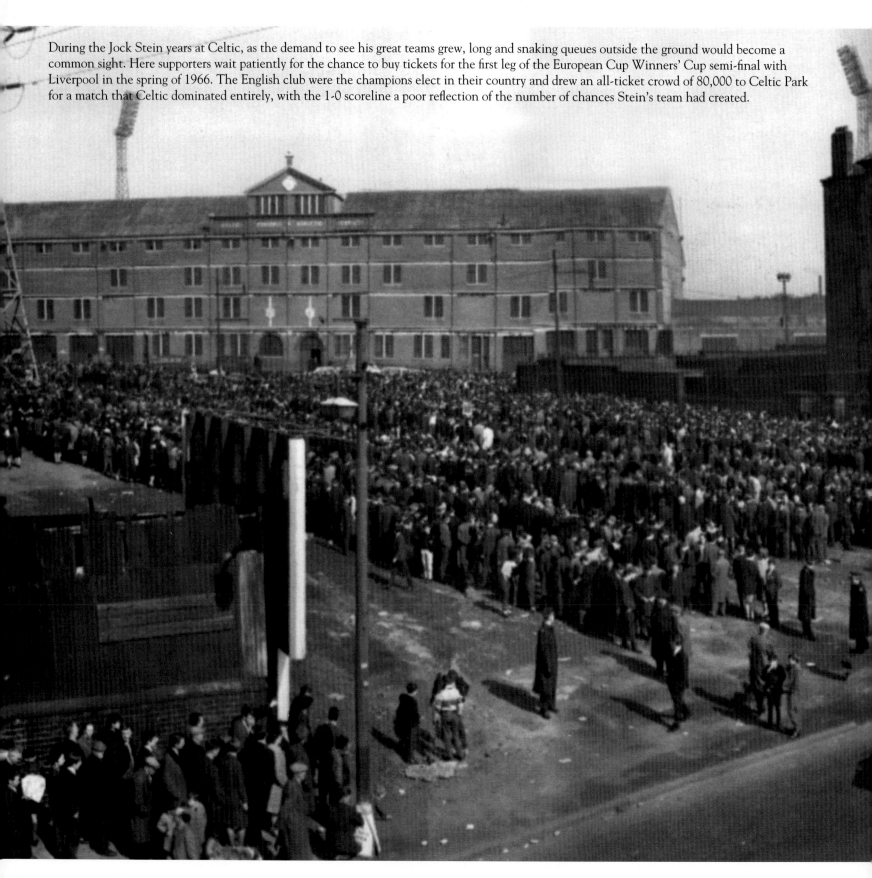

ABOVE: Tommy Gemmell turns photographer as Celtic settle in at their hotel in Southport prior to the second leg of the European Cup Winners' Cup semi-final with Liverpool at Anfield in April 1966. Victims of the budding snapper are Ian Young (left), Gemmell's fellow full-back, Ronnie Simpson, the goalkeeper, and John Fallon, the reserve goalkeeper.

LEFT: Bobby Lennox, Jimmy Johnstone and John Hughes lead the despondent Celtic players as they arrive back in Glasgow after the second-leg defeat to Liverpool in the 1966 European Cup Winners' Cup semi-final. Liverpool had won 2-0 at Anfield for a 2-1 aggregate victory but close to the end Lennox had the ball in the net only to be ruled, incorrectly, to have been offside. The speed, timing and anticipation of Lennox would often catch officials out and this defeat was felt bitterly by the Celtic players, especially as the final was that year scheduled for Hampden Park.

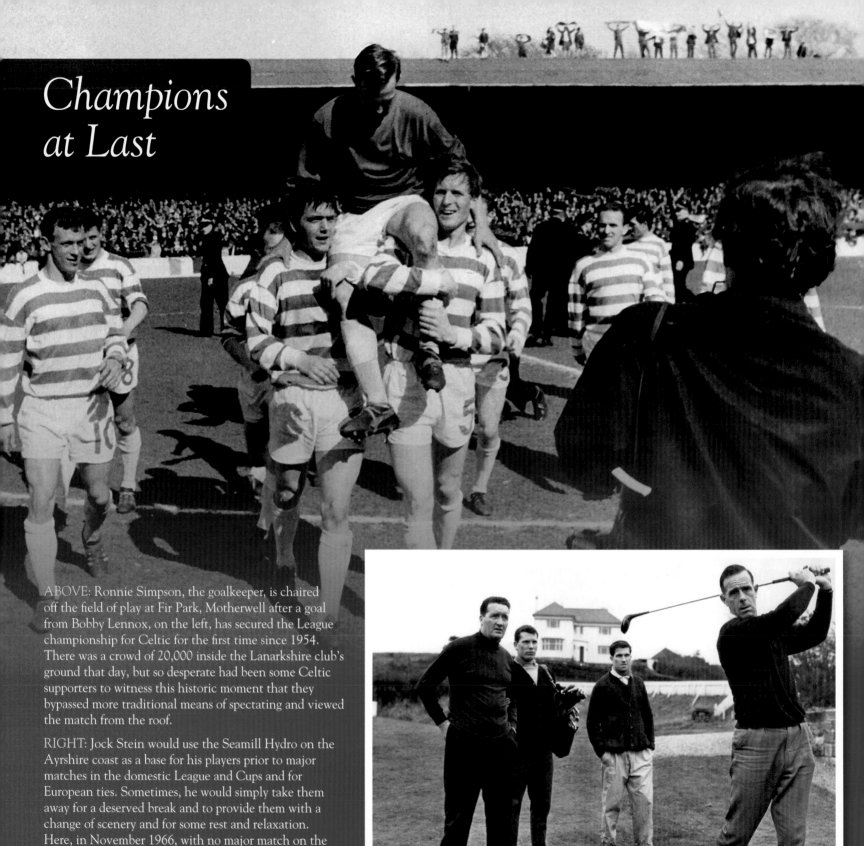

Champions at Last

ABOVE: Ronnie Simpson, the goalkeeper, is chaired off the field of play at Fir Park, Motherwell after a goal from Bobby Lennox, on the left, has secured the League championship for Celtic for the first time since 1954. There was a crowd of 20,000 inside the Lanarkshire club's ground that day, but so desperate had been some Celtic supporters to witness this historic moment that they bypassed more traditional means of spectating and viewed the match from the roof.

RIGHT: Jock Stein would use the Seamill Hydro on the Ayrshire coast as a base for his players prior to major matches in the domestic League and Cups and for European ties. Sometimes, he would simply take them away for a deserved break and to provide them with a change of scenery and for some rest and relaxation. Here, in November 1966, with no major match on the horizon, Stein allows his men to unwind on the golf course. Ronnie Simpson, an expert golfer, tees off, with Stein, Joe McBride and Bertie Auld watching the ball.

A stupendous shot from Jimmy Johnstone, who had veered infield to the edge of the Rangers penalty area, puts Celtic 2-1 ahead at Ibrox in the League title decider for the 1966-7 season. The match finished 2-2 but that was enough for Celtic to clinch the championship.

Celtic players at the Scottish Television studios in December 1966 for an exclusive live screening of the match between Liverpool and Ajax Amsterdam, their possible opponents in the quarter-finals; the draw for which was to be made on the following day. Ajax would triumph in this encounter but Celtic's opponents in the quarter-finals would prove to be Vojvodina Novi Sad of Yugoslavia, and although Celtic would win 2-1 on aggregate, many members of the team regarded the Yugoslavs as the toughest opponents they faced in the 1966-7 European Cup.

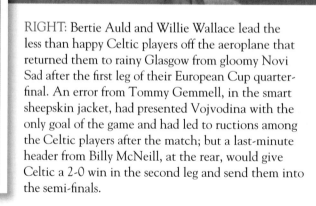

RIGHT: Bertie Auld and Willie Wallace lead the less than happy Celtic players off the aeroplane that returned them to rainy Glasgow from gloomy Novi Sad after the first leg of their European Cup quarter-final. An error from Tommy Gemmell, in the smart sheepskin jacket, had presented Vojvodina with the only goal of the game and had led to ructions among the Celtic players after the match; but a last-minute header from Billy McNeill, at the rear, would give Celtic a 2-0 win in the second leg and send them into the semi-finals.

ABOVE: Tommy Gemmell, sartorially elegant, as always, in January 1967 by strange coincidence shows off a lucky pennant of Internazionale of Milan, the club against whom he would score Celtic's opening goal in the final of the European Cup four months later. Gemmell, a player who successfully married consistency with explosive unpredictability, was, that January, on the eve of making his 100th consecutive appearance for Celtic, in a match against St Johnstone in Perth. That match would also be significant in that it would be the first time that the team that would become known as the Lisbon Lions would be fielded together; in a match that Celtic would win 4-0.

Willie Wallace, who scored two of the three goals in the 3-1 first-leg European Cup semi-final victory over Dukla Prague, challenges for the ball in the match with the Czechs at Celtic Park.

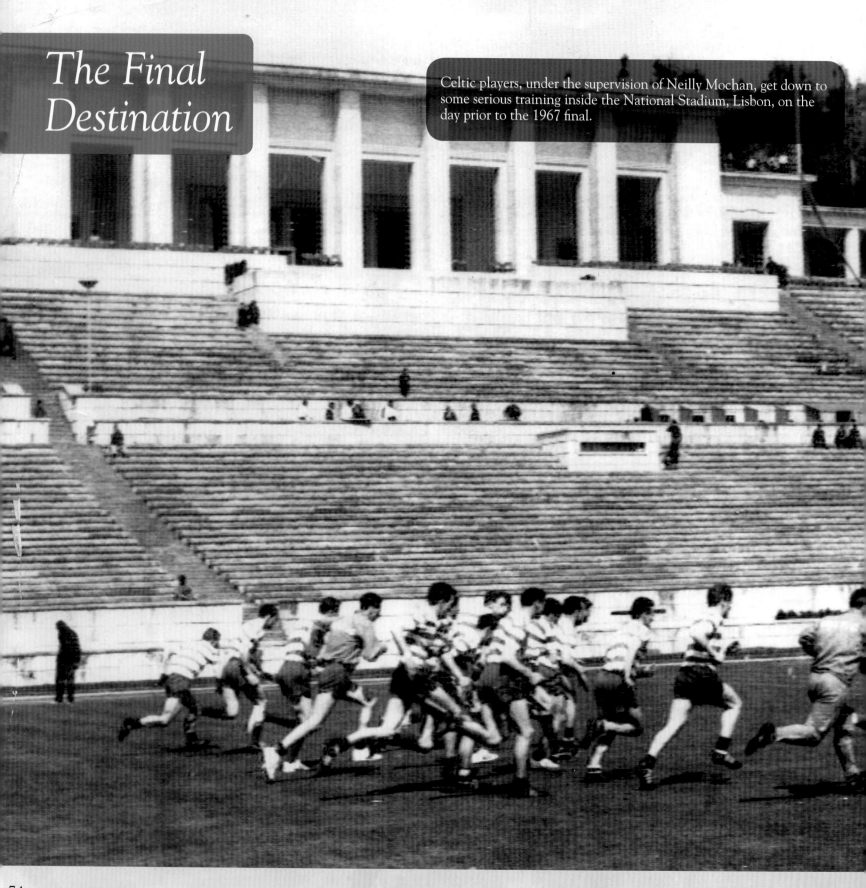

The Final Destination

Celtic players, under the supervision of Neilly Mochan, get down to some serious training inside the National Stadium, Lisbon, on the day prior to the 1967 final.

A visit to the National Stadium, Lisbon, on the day before the final for, from left to right: Stevie Chalmers, Ian Young, Billy McNeill, Jimmy Johnstone and Bobby Lennox. The venue was perhaps the most unusual ever to be used for a European Cup final. Unlike most major stadiums, it was not set in a densely populated area but amidst woodland six miles outside the city and with one side of the ground not only tree-lined but, as seen in the background here, with a tiny stand that would not have been out of place in the Scottish second division. There would still be a 56,000 crowd inside the stadium for the final.

LEFT: One of the precious, beautifully designed tickets for the 1967 European Cup final. The design incorporated an image of the old-style European Cup, which Real Madrid had retained after winning it for the sixth time in 1966. Celtic and Internazionale would be contesting a new trophy, one with a long, streamlined, convex body and with wide, elongated handles, which would become the classic European trophy.

75

Celtic players rush to congratulate Tommy Gemmell, the Celtic number three, after he had scored Celtic's equaliser in the 1967 final, while shocked Internazionale players are left reeling in the wake of his strike.

The *Daily Record* reports Celtic's victory in Lisbon.

–LEGENDS–

Stevie Chalmers

A typically subtle and stylish finish from Stevie Chalmers provided Celtic with the most important goal in the club's history. Five minutes from full-time in the 1967 European Cup final, Bobby Murdoch sent a low, hard ball into the Internazionale penalty area and Chalmers extended his right boot to get just enough on the ball to send it past Giuliano Sarti in the Italian team's goal. It was a goal that combined economy of effort with expert positioning and it was entirely typical in style of a man who is the fourth-highest goalscorer in Celtic's history.

Not only could Stevie Chalmers score goals in a good team, such as the Lisbon Lions, but he had also done so, prolifically, in the series of struggling teams fielded by Celtic during the first half of the 1960s. A highly disciplined player and a gentleman, Chalmers would be the leading scorer for Celtic in the glorious 1966-7 season and after a decade at the club, his final flourish would come with the superb fourth goal against Rangers in the 4-0 victory in the 1969 Scottish Cup final; when he once again put the ball in the net in his characteristically neat, deceptively easy-looking fashion.

> "A modest and hard-working guy but a magnificent goalscorer.
>
> Bobby Lennox on Stevie Chalmers
> "

FOOTBALL –STATS–

Stevie Chalmers

Name: Stephen Chalmers

Born: 1936

Playing Career: 1959–1975

Clubs: Celtic, Morton, Partick Thistle

Celtic Appearances: 405

Goals: 231

Scotland Appearances: 5

Goals: 3

ABOVE: A more mature Stevie Chalmers (left) shows off the European Cup trophy with Tommy Gemmell, his fellow Celtic goalscorer in the 1967 final.

Stevie Chalmers, in the number nine shorts, turns away after scoring the winning goal in Lisbon.

Willie Wallace, the Celtic forward, is lifted in celebration by happy Portuguese and Scottish fans at the conclusion of Celtic's momentous victory in Lisbon.

Celtic deserved their victory. It was a victory for sport.

Helenio Herrera, manager of Internazionale

81

The Ultimate Victory

Liz McNeill (left) and Anne Deas, the fiancée of Tommy Gemmell, the latter wearing a specially designed green-and-white hooped coat for the occasion, disembark in Glasgow from the aeroplane that had carried the players' partners back from Lisbon on the day after the European Cup final.

Two ball boys transporting the European Cup around the track at Celtic Park on the occasion of the first competitive home game after Lisbon, a rain-drenched League Cup tie with Dundee United in August 1967 that drew 54,000 and in which the Lisbon Lions were fielded, with Jimmy Johnstone winning the match for Celtic with the only goal of the game. Here the great trophy is on its way past the enclosure in front of the main stand.

ABOVE: A fortnight after Celtic's victory in Lisbon, Stein's team travelled to Madrid to face Real in the testimonial match for Alfredo di Stefano. This was no end-of-season friendly but a tough contest, a grudge match, with representatives of Real disparaging Celtic in the Spanish press in the days before the game and claiming that they, the European champions in 1966, were still the premier team in Europe. The game was so fierily competitive that Bertie Auld and Amancio, Real's star player, were sent off and Bobby Lennox suffered particularly tough treatment from the Real defence. Here Lennox, in front of a packed Bernabeu Stadium, provides the ultimate response by scoring the only goal of the game and silencing Celtic's Spanish critics.

Celtic participated in another prestigious occasion in the autumn of 1967 when they faced Racing Club of Buenos Aires, the South American champions, in the World Clubs Cup, the intercontinental two-legged competition to decide the club world champions. It proved another testing evening for Celtic, with the Argentinean players employing vicious underhand tactics, such as spitting, pulling hair and gouging eyes, to put their opponents off their game. The first leg, in Glasgow, was played at Hampden Park to accommodate a crowd of 90,000 and here Billy McNeill rises into the air to score the only goal of that game.

Madness and Mayhem

Celtic players (below) training at the Avellaneda Stadium, Buenos Aires, before the second leg of the World Clubs Cup encounter with Racing Club. There were 1,000 policemen on duty on the day of the game to control an Argentinean crowd that was in furious mood.

LEFT: Ronnie Simpson, the Celtic goalkeeper, receives some help from Neilly Mochan, the trainer, after having been struck by a missile thrown from behind his goal prior to the second leg of the tie between Celtic and Racing Club at the Avellaneda Stadium in Buenos Aires. The cut to his head that Simpson received during the warm-up forced him to pull out of a match that would again be pockmarked by numerous examples of Argentinean gamesmanship, and although Celtic scored first through a Tommy Gemmell penalty, Racing won 2-1 to force a play-off in Montevideo, Uruguay, on 4th November 1967.

BELOW: Uruguayan security forces attempt to restrain Alfio Basile of Racing Club following his dismissal in tandem with Celtic's Bobby Lennox during the play-off for the World Clubs Cup in Montevideo in November 1967, a match that descended at times into serious violence on the field. Rodolfo Osorio, the referee, lost control and at one stage, as the match became ever more turbulent, called the two captains together and told them that the next time there was an incident of any sort, the number six of Racing and eight of Celtic would be dismissed, even if it did not involve them. This duly happened and may explain the outrage felt by Basile, who would later manage the Argentina national team. Two players from Racing Club and four from Celtic were dismissed in a chaotic match that Racing won 1-0 to claim a tarnished trophy.

The Stein Scene
1968-1978

> " We always felt we could beat anybody.
>
> Davie Hay "

A fine blend of experienced and promising Celtic talents look out on a promising new decade from their hotel in Harrogate before the first leg of the 1970 European Cup semi-final with Leeds United.

1968 Kenny Dalglish makes his Celtic debut as a substitute in a 4-2 win at Hamilton Academical. 1969 Celtic complete their second treble, defeating Hibernian 6-2 in the League Cup final and Rangers 4-0 in the Scottish Cup final. 1970 A second European Cup final appearance sees Celtic lose 2-1 to Feyenoord of Holland. 1971 Celtic pip Aberdeen to the League title and equal the record of six successive League titles set by the Celtic team of 1904-10. 1972 Internazionale win a European Cup semi-final on penalties as Celtic lose in their first shootout. 1973 Lou Macari becomes the first Celt transferred for a six-figure sum when he moves to Manchester United for £200,000. 1974 Celtic establish a record by winning their ninth successive Scottish League title. 1975 Jock Stein narrowly escapes death after a car crash on the M74 and is forced to take a year away from football management to recuperate. Billy McNeill retires and Jimmy Johnstone is allowed to leave Celtic. 1977 Celtic win the Premier Division for the first time since League reconstruction and complete the double by beating Rangers in the Scottish Cup final. Kenny Dalglish is transferred from Celtic to Liverpool for a British record transfer fee of £440,000. 1978 Jock Stein quits as Celtic manager to be replaced by Billy McNeill.

Jock Stein roars his approval as Celtic beat Leeds United 2-1 at Hampden Park in April 1970 and ensure a place in their second European Cup final.

Bobby Murdoch and Billy McNeill look back in sorrow at the end of the European Cup quarter-final with Milan in March 1969. After a 0-0 draw in Italy, Celtic were eliminated by a Pierino Prati goal in the return at Celtic Park.

A happier European occasion for Billy McNeill as he beats José Henrique, the Benfica goalkeeper, to the ball to send a header only narrowly over the bar. Celtic would still win this November 1969 European Cup tie at Celtic Park by 3-0.

Extracurricular Activities

The Celtic players of the 1960s were a tight-knit bunch and would regularly meet for parties in each other's homes. Here John Hughes, Jimmy Johnstone, John Clark and Bobby Murdoch and partners gather for their Christmas party in December 1969.

BELOW: Celtic and Rangers meet in less tempestuous circumstances than usual as players from the two clubs participate in BBC Television's *Quiz Ball* programme. Play would progress up the pitch in the direction of the opposing team's goal with each answer that the participants got correct. Celtic's Willie Wallace, Jim Craig and Billy McNeill are being assisted in this December 1969 episode by John Cairney, the actor, who proved a most accomplished member of the team; while the Rangers players John Greig, Jim Baxter and Dave Smith have as team guest the songwriter Bill Martin. *Quiz Ball* was screened across Britain and involved clubs from Scotland and England. Celtic won the 1969-70 competition by beating Heart of Midlothian in an all-Scottish final and went on to win the 1970 Champions Series by defeating Everton 7-5 in the final after having beaten Aberdeen (right) 4-3 in the semi..

ABOVE: Ronnie Simpson, the Celtic goalkeeper (second from right) in 1970 became a Conservative councillor for Edinburgh's upmarket Corstorphine ward, where he was elected with a majority of 2,300.

WILLIE WALLACE

JIM CRAIG

JOHN CAIRNEY

BILLY M

CELTIC

It's the 1970 European Cup final and Willie Wallace and Eddy Pieters Graafland, the Feyenoord goalkeeper, watch the ball whirr in the direction of the Dutch team's goal. The match in Milan would prove to be a devastating one for Celtic as Feyenoord won the final 2-1, despite having been as much the underdogs in 1970 as Celtic had been in the match with Internazionale in 1967.

Celtic's defeat was especially hard to take in that they had defeated a slew of illustrious and tough opponents to get to the final, including Benfica, the Portuguese champions, Fiorentina, the Italian champions, and Leeds United, the leading team in England. The match with Leeds was particularly lustrous, with Celtic widely written off in the English press as having no chance against Don Revie's supposedly invincible team; but in both legs of the tie Celtic outplayed and out-thought those much-vaunted opponents.

Feyenoord, in contrast, were largely unheralded, as Dutch football in 1970 entirely lacked the pedigree it would later develop. There were recriminations after the final, with all sorts of rumours and supposed reasons for the defeat swirling around, but perhaps the most significant aspect was that George Connelly, who had been outstanding in stiffening the three-man Celtic midfield against Leeds, was dropped to the substitutes' bench for the final – and it was in midfield that Feyenoord proved to be especially strong.

Celtic and Feyenoord supporters in exuberant form before the 1970 final as they cram into the central Piazza del Duomo in Milan.

Willie Wallace, Bobby Lennox, Billy McNeill and George Connelly, the substitute, look utterly despondent after the defeat to Feyenoord.

TERMOZETA

—LEGENDS—

The ball at his toe, Jimmy Johnstone prepares to guide it away from Tommy McLean, of Rangers, a fellow winger, in a match at Ibrox in the autumn of 1971.

Jimmy Johnstone

No player has ever captured the imagination of the Celtic support more fully or colourfully than Jimmy Johnstone. The winger seemed to encapsulate what Celtic is all about – skill, unpredictability and a wonderfully entertaining approach to the task of winning football matches. Johnstone was a vital component of the Celtic team between the mid-1960s and mid-1970s – and it is not coincidental that this was the club's most successful decade. His brilliance could unlock the most seemingly impermeable defences in an instant.

Johnstone was one of several players who owed much to Jock Stein for effecting a dramatic turnaround in their careers. Although his close control and ball-juggling skills had always amazed his team-mates, he was lingering in the reserves when Stein arrived at the club as manager in 1965 and, for the next 10 years, much coaxing and cajoling from the manager would keep Jimmy as close to the straight and narrow as possible. The player, in return, was a magnificent matchwinner for his manager.

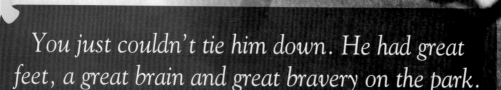

You just couldn't tie him down. He had great feet, a great brain and great bravery on the park.

Danny McGrain on Jimmy Johnstone

98

It was as a mesmerising dribbler of the ball that Jimmy Johnstone earned worldwide fame and adulation, but he also had a great spring and could score tremendous goals with his head, despite his diminutive size. Here, in the 1970 Scottish Cup final, he rises to challenge Bobby Clark, the Aberdeen goalkeeper, for the ball.

FOOTBALL
–STATS–

Jimmy Johnstone

Name: James Johnstone

Born: 1944

Died: 2006

Playing Career: 1961–1979

Clubs: Celtic, San José Earthquakes, Sheffield United, Dundee, Shelbourne, Elgin City

Celtic Appearances: 515

Goals: 130

Scotland Appearances: 23

Goals: 4

Two greats together as Johan Cruyff is introduced by Jimmy to James, the Celtic winger's son.

The Heavy Team

John Hughes leads Tommy Gemmell through a testing series of obstacles during pre-season training. The heftier players in Jock Stein's squad, such as Hughes and Gemmell, were nicknamed by the manager as the "heavy team" and would be put through their own, extra demanding, training programme every summer.

Bobby Murdoch (left) and Dixie Deans, a striker signed in October 1971, were both susceptible to putting on extra weight. Murdoch's weight fluctuated so worryingly that Jock Stein would send him to a health farm in England to try to control it.

Dixie in lighter mood as he participates in a blow-football match with John Brownlie of Hibernian.

Seasoned Travellers

ABOVE: Celtic supporters with a specially customised car to take them to the continent and the European Cup final with Milan in 1970.

RIGHT: Tommy Gemmell, the most extrovert among Jock Stein's players, larks around with an Air France stewardess, happily pinning a green rosette on her uniform, the joke being that the stewardesses' blue outfits would have to be modified for the purposes of carrying Celtic abroad.

It would perhaps be stretching the truth to describe Elizabeth Taylor as a Celtic supporter but the actress proved happy to join in the fun when, in 1972, she and Richard Burton, her husband, at that time Hollywood's most celebrated couple, threw a £5,000 victory party to celebrate Celtic's European Cup victory over Ujpest Dozsa: the couple's visit to Budapest had coincided with Celtic's trip to the city.

Jock Stein disapproved of his players being associated in any way with alcohol, but he was not averse to using beer crates to improvise a training routine, as here with Davie Hay, a player who thrust his way into the Celtic team during the early 1970s.

LEFT: It may look like another of Stein's unusual training exercises but the reason he has his players scaling this wall in the environs of Seamill Hydro is that the door in the wall that led back to the team's accommodation had been locked.

RIGHT: Jimmy Johnstone and John Hughes, shuttling in opposite directions, pass Stein during another intense training session.

Stein never lost his appetite for training and the players would testify that throughout his time at the club he brought a zest and a drive to their preparations on the practice field that served them well when it came to matches. Here, Harry Hood, under the demanding gaze of Stein, moves on to the ball during a session in Troon.

A Circus Act

ABOVE: Celtic and Internazionale prepare to do battle again in the second leg of their 1972 European Cup semi-final at Celtic Park. Billy McNeill, the Celtic captain, exchanges pennants with Sandro Mazzola, Inter's captain in 1972 and the Italian side's goalscorer in the final between the clubs five years previously.

ABOVE: The Celtic players mill around prior to the penalty shootout after the match with Inter had concluded in a 0-0 draw after extra-time, making a scoreless aggregate after a 0-0 draw in the first leg. It would be Celtic's first participation in a shootout and after they lost 5-4 in an innovation that had been introduced to European football only in 1970, Jock Stein described this process of settling a match as "a circus act".

RIGHT: The disappointment of defeat is clear on the face of Lou Macari after the penalty defeat to Inter.

An anxious Celtic crowd, resplendent in the hairstyles of the early 1970s, wonder what is going to happen next as Bobby Davidson, the referee, confers with Jim Renton, his linesman, before calling over Jim Hermiston, the Aberdeen left-back, and Jimmy Johnstone, the Celtic winger, following an altercation between the two players during the Scottish Cup quarter-final at Celtic Park in March 1973.

LEFT: Hermiston receives a ticking off but is allowed to continue while (below) Johnstone, to his consternation, is dismissed.

Fresh Faces

Dale and Lou Macari, a handsome young couple, step out in the sunshine in 1972. Macari, in January 1973, would be the first of a talented batch of young Celts known collectively as the Quality Street Gang, to leave the club, when, after agitating for a transfer, he switched to Manchester United for a £200,000 fee.

ABOVE: Marina and Kenny Dalglish beam with happiness on their wedding day in November 1974.

LEFT: George Connelly scrutinizes the Player of the Year trophy that he was awarded in the spring of 1974. The talented young midfield player, who was prone to going AWOL from Celtic Park and Scotland squads, walked out on Celtic and top-level football for the final time in 1975, at the age of 26.

Dixie Deans squeezes the ball past Jim McArthur, the Hibernian goalkeeper, to score in Celtic's 3-0 victory at Easter Road in April 1973, a win that secured an eighth successive championship for Celtic on the last day of the season in front of a 45,000 crowd.

It's Still Seamill

The use of Seamill Hydro made for a bracing environment whenever Celtic players travelled there to prepare for a major match, especially during the winter. Here Peter Latchford, the English goalkeeper who joined the club from West Bromwich Albion, accompanies Bobby Lennox and Kenny Dalglish on a stroll along the Ayrshire seafront in November 1975 as the team prepares for a European Cup Winners' Cup tie with Boavista of Portugal. The two Scots are either feeling the effects of the elements more severely than Latchford or are better adjusted to coping with them than the affable goalkeeper, who had arrived at the club only that year.

Johannes Edvaldsson, the Iceland international centre-back, and another well-loved import, who, like Latchford, arrived in 1975, scores the second goal against Boavista in the 3-1 victory on Guy Fawkes Night 1975 that sent Celtic into the quarter-finals of the European Cup Winners' Cup. Dixie Deans and Kenny Dalglish (far left and far right respectively) are the onlooking Celts.

Putting on the Style

Danny McGrain, Kenny Dalglish, Harry Hood and Tommy Callaghan show varying degrees of pleasure at being asked to parade the latest in mid-1970s fashions at Celtic Park.

–LEGENDS–

Billy McNeill

It was Jock Stein who insisted upon Celtic signing Billy McNeill after the then reserve-team coach had watched him perform for Scotland against England in a schoolboy international at Celtic Park, which the home side won. When Stein later returned to Celtic as manager in 1965, McNeill, who had been on the verge of a lucrative move to Tottenham Hotspur, knew how much potential the new manager had and happily dedicated the rest of his playing career to a club that he had never really wished to leave. McNeill was the keystone in Stein's great teams, not only as a tough, utterly committed centre-half but as the quintessential team captain.

McNeill's desire to urge his team-mates on to greater things was self-evident, and he would also lead by example. He only rarely scored goals but when he did they tended to be vital ones. It was McNeill who headed the spectacular winner against Dunfermline Athletic in the 1965 Scottish Cup final to secure Stein's first trophy as Celtic manager and it was McNeill again who rose into the air in the final minute of the European Cup quarter-final with the doughty Vojvodina Novi Sad to head the goal that put Celtic into the semis. Billy McNeill was a huge presence and an essential element in Celtic's greatest era.

Billy McNeill expertly ushers Zoltan Varga, the Aberdeen player, away from goal, during an encounter with the side from the north-east in March 1972.

" *He was a terrific centre-half and the mainstay of the team.*

Bobby Lennox
"

Billy McNeill chats with Kevin Keegan and Emlyn Hughes of Liverpool prior to McNeill's testimonial against the English club in 1974. It was a great source of pleasure to McNeill that Celtic's standing during his time at the club was such that they could feel on an equal footing with the great European clubs such as Liverpool and the giants of Italy and Spain.

LEFT: Jock Stein and Bill Shankly, the Liverpool manager, chat with McNeill. A dominant, enthusiastic and inspirational figure on the field of play, McNeill, as his playing career reached its final years in the 1970s, appeared a natural successor to Stein.

FOOTBALL –STATS–

Billy McNeill

Name: William McNeill

Born: 1940

Playing Career: 1957–1975

Clubs: Celtic

Celtic Appearances: 790

Goals: 35

Scotland Appearances: 29

Goals: 3

Managerial career: 1977-1991

Clubs: Clyde, Aberdeen, Celtic, Manchester City, Aston Villa, Celtic

Billy McNeill prepares to challenge Johan Cruyff for the ball during a 1971 European Cup quarter-final in Amsterdam.

Kenny Dalglish (far left), with typical grace and balance, heads the second goal in a 2-0 victory over Partick Thistle in February 1977 to keep Celtic comfortably top of the League. Jock Stein had struggled to adjust to football management again after returning in 1976 from his year's recuperation following his car accident, but the team that was seeking to win the double in 1977 was a refined, well-balanced one that did credit to the manager.

—LEGENDS—

Kenny Dalglish

A powerful case can be constructed to suggest that Kenny Dalglish is not only the greatest Scottish footballer of all but the greatest British one too. Such disputatious claims can never be fully resolved, but those who saw Dalglish perform with unstinting excellence year after year for Celtic, Liverpool and Scotland undoubtedly saw a unique player, a British equivalent of Johan Cruyff, the great Dutchman and the finest European player of all. Dalglish lacked the type of speed over the ground with which Cruyff was blessed but he was his equal as a footballer in every other way.

A prize goalscorer, who also specialized in making chances for team-mates, Dalglish scored all sorts of goals, usually clever, often spectacular, through his sharp assessment of angles and openings in opposing defences. He had become, by the mid-1970s, one of the most prized talents in the British game and when he, the last of The Quality Street gang to insist upon a move, left Celtic for Liverpool in August 1977, his departure tore a hole in the club from which, it could be argued, Celtic have still not entirely recovered.

Kenny Dalglish, here making his full debut against Raith Rovers in October 1969, always displayed the same competitive edge in training as he did on matchday. That professionalism, allied to his innate talent, would take him far in the game.

> " He took a lot of knocks and got a lot of goals that lesser people who were not as brave as him would not have.
>
> Jimmy Johnstone

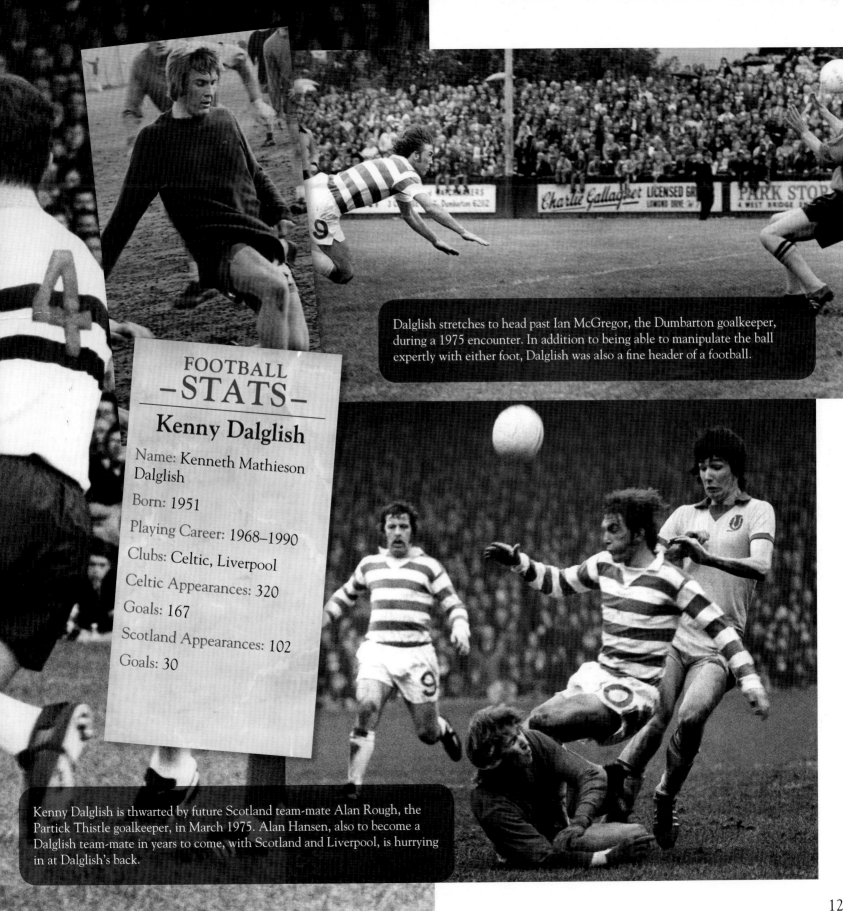

FOOTBALL -STATS-

Kenny Dalglish

Name: Kenneth Mathieson Dalglish

Born: 1951

Playing Career: 1968–1990

Clubs: Celtic, Liverpool

Celtic Appearances: 320

Goals: 167

Scotland Appearances: 102

Goals: 30

Dalglish stretches to head past Ian McGregor, the Dumbarton goalkeeper, during a 1975 encounter. In addition to being able to manipulate the ball expertly with either foot, Dalglish was also a fine header of a football.

Kenny Dalglish is thwarted by future Scotland team-mate Alan Rough, the Partick Thistle goalkeeper, in March 1975. Alan Hansen, also to become a Dalglish team-mate in years to come, with Scotland and Liverpool, is hurrying in at Dalglish's back.

Switching Sides

Alfie Conn eases the ball away from a challenge in an encounter with his former team shortly after the midfield player, who had featured for Rangers in the early 1970s, had joined Celtic from Tottenham Hotspur in early 1977.

The transfer of Alfie Conn from Tottenham Hotspur to Celtic said [mu]ch about where Celtic stood in the late 1970s and about the [co]ncluding phase of Jock Stein's management of the club. The move [wa]s sensationalized because Conn had previously played for Rangers [and] superficially this looked like one of the many publicity coups that [had] been characteristic of Stein in pushing Celtic to the fore at the [exp]ense of their great rivals. Conn, however, appeared to be no longer [quit]e as good a player as he had been at Ibrox and the fee of £65,000 [was] considerably lower than those that Celtic had taken in from the [big-]figure transfers of such players as Lou Macari and David Hay to [Engl]and. Regardless of the sizeable fees for which his better players [were] sold, it seemed that Stein would never be given similar amounts to [stren]gthen his team following the loss of such talents. It looked like a [recip]e for consistently reduced standards.

ABOVE: Alfie Conn prepares to lose the luxuriant mane, characteristic of the 1970s, that he had worn at Tottenham Hotspur but which was never likely to meet with the approval of Jock Stein, who always liked his players to look neat and tidy.

RIGHT: Alfie, shorn of his locks and beard, prepares to do his bit for Celtic.

—LEGENDS—

Bobby Lennox

The perfect professional footballer, Bobby Lennox combined a dedication to fitness and practice with an optimistic personality and exceptional, explosive talent as a goalscoring winger of the highest order. His outstanding pace, awareness and powers of anticipation meant that he could burst through defences using his acceleration and carry the ball through either to score speedily or to create chances for others. He was also expert at anticipating loose balls inside the penalty area and would eagerly scoop up close-range goals from rebounds or from mayhem caused inside panicked defences.

Bobby's enthusiasm for the game, dedicated approach and first-class fitness combined to make him Celtic's highest post-war goalscorer. The only minor regret that the even-tempered Lennox harbours about his career is that he was not played through the middle more often than on the wing, where he habitually found himself. If he had featured more centrally, many more goals than his already awesome haul would almost certainly have come his way.

> *One of the finest strikers I've ever seen. He was brilliant.*
>
> Bobby Charlton on Bobby Lennox

Bobby Lennox, in a 1976 European Cup Winners' Cup tie with Sachsenring Zwickau of East Germany, displays the determination, balance and drive that made him such a tremendous goalscorer for Celtic.

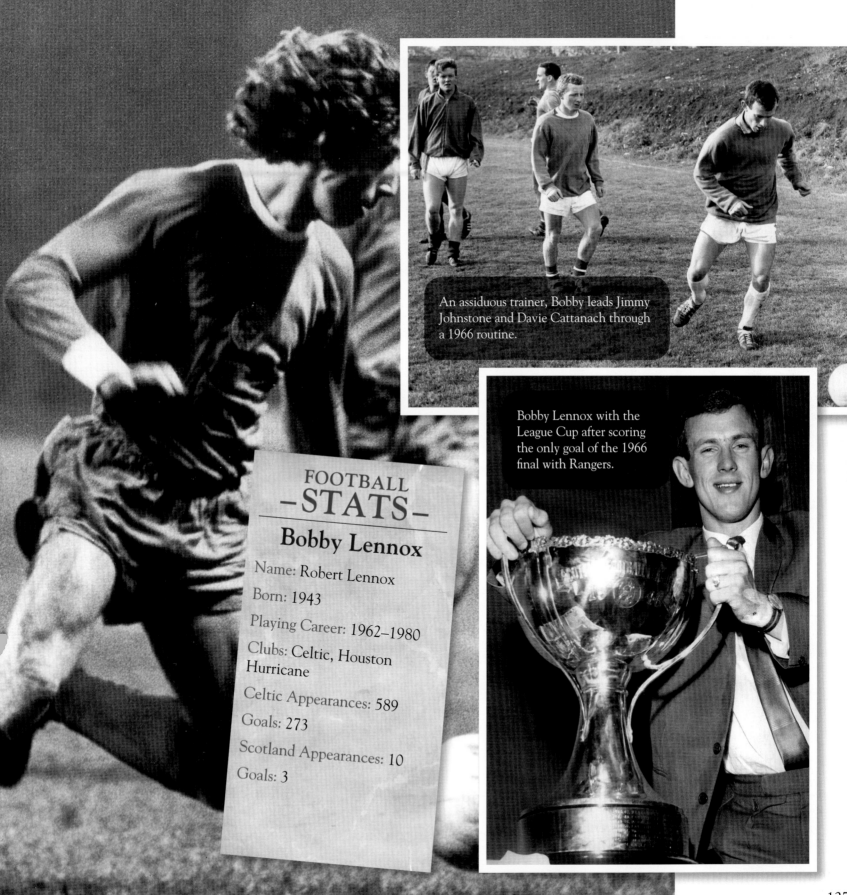

An assiduous trainer, Bobby leads Jimmy Johnstone and Davie Cattanach through a 1966 routine.

Bobby Lennox with the League Cup after scoring the only goal of the 1966 final with Rangers.

FOOTBALL
–STATS–
Bobby Lennox

Name: Robert Lennox

Born: 1943

Playing Career: 1962–1980

Clubs: Celtic, Houston Hurricane

Celtic Appearances: 589

Goals: 273

Scotland Appearances: 10

Goals: 3

Roddie MacDonald, the Celtic centre-back, watches the ball elude Hamish McAlpine, the Dundee United goalkeeper, in a tense encounter at Celtic Park in March 1977. The Tannadice club had pursued Celtic closely for the title all season and they and Aberdeen were providing a serious challenge to the Glasgow side that they would sustain into the 1980s.

A Farewell Double

Roy Baines, the Celtic goalkeeper, makes a noteworthy stop from a Dundee United penalty-kick, taken by Hamish McAlpine, the United goalkeeper, in the background. It kept the score at 0-0 in the crucial League match at Celtic Park in 1977, which Celtic would go on to win 2-0, a victory that made the Premier Division title all but theirs.

ABOVE: Peter Latchford consoles Kenny Dalglish after the 1977 Scottish Cup final. Celtic had won, beating Rangers 1-0 through an Andy Lynch penalty. In the aftermath of the match, Dalglish lost his winner's medal, which made him despondent: but the medal was later discovered inside an umbrella, and Kenny's good humour was instantly restored.

LEFT: Jock Stein congratulates Kenny Dalglish after the 1977 Scottish Cup final. It would be their final triumph together as, much to Stein's regret, Dalglish would opt to leave for Liverpool that summer.

—LEGENDS—

Jock Stein

"Oh that's fantastic. Wait and see how things change now." Billy McNeill's words on hearing of Jock Stein's appointment as Celtic manager were endorsed by the new man's impact on the club but even McNeill could never have predicted just how magnificent Stein's achievements with Celtic would turn out to be. Within two years of taking over a team that had grown used to failure, he had transformed that set of players, with only a couple of additions, into the champions of Europe.

Stein's innovative grasp of tactics, his use of players in their strongest positions and his ability to make his men fear him enormously whilst simultaneously wishing to please him as much as they could, made him one of the most formidable managerial figures the British game has seen. The 25 trophies that he amassed in his 13 years as Celtic manager only tells part of the tale. Those trophies were won by Celtic teams playing with wit and verve, invention and style and for Stein to insist that Celtic not only won, but won well, makes him special.

Jock Stein makes his feelings known from the bench as Jimmy Johnstone, watched by Bobby Lennox, receives a booking in a match with Hibernian at Easter Road in 1970.

> " *It was as close to a miracle as management can go.* "
>
> Sir Alex Ferguson on Jock Stein leading Celtic to their European Cup triumph in 1967

RIGHT: A hug for Eddie Turnbull, the Aberdeen manager, shows the affection Jock Stein would have for those within his business whose achievements and managerial style he respected.

BELOW: Jock Stein is flanked by Billy McNeill and John Clark, his former players, outside Celtic Park on the day in 1978 when he relinquished the role of Celtic manager that he had held for 13 years. He was to be succeeded by McNeill, whom Stein had first approached with the suggestion that McNeill become his successor.

FOOTBALL -STATS-

Jock Stein

Name: John Stein

Born: 1922

Died: 1985

Playing Career: 1942–1957

Clubs: Albion Rovers, Llanelli, Celtic

Celtic Appearances: 148

Goals: 2

Managerial Career: 1960-1985

Clubs: Dunfermline Athletic, Hibernian, Celtic, Leeds United, also Scotland national team

Jock Stein hugs Jimmy Johnstone as he and some of his former players appear on the pitch at Celtic Park in August 1978 prior to Stein's testimonial match with Liverpool.

" *We had players who could make passes, players who could keep the ball. We could defend. We could score goals. We had a good blend in midfield. We had everything.*

Murdo MacLeod on Celtic in the 1980s "

Murdo MacLeod is crowded out by most of the Nottingham Forest team as he takes a free-kick in the 1983 UEFA Cup tie with the English side.

1979 Celtic win the Premier Division title in dramatic style by defeating Rangers 4-2 in the final match of the season. 1980 Following Celtic's 1-0 victory over Rangers in the Scottish Cup final, a riot breaks out at Hampden Park. 1981 Dundee United eliminate Celtic from both the 1980-1 season Cup competitions but Celtic win the League title at Tannadice in April. 1982 A 3-0 victory over St Mirren sees Celtic win the League title on the final day of the season. 1983 Charlie Nicholas scores 48 goals in the 1982-3 season but leaves for Arsenal for a reported fee of £650,000. 1984 Rapid Vienna cheat Celtic out of their due place in the quarter-finals of the European Cup Winners' Cup after Rudi Weinhofer feigns injury and the Austrian club persuade UEFA to replay the second leg that Celtic had won comfortably. 1985 Spectacular late goals from Davie Provan and Frank McGarvey see Celtic come from behind to defeat Dundee United 2-1 in the centenary Scottish Cup final. 1986 Another dramatic final day of the season sees Celtic win 5-0 at St Mirren to pip Heart of Midlothian to the title. 1987 David Hay becomes the first Celtic manager to be sacked rather than resign and after a four-year absence Billy McNeill returns to Celtic. 1988 Celtic celebrate their centenary year by winning the League and Cup double in magnificent fashion. 1989 Dariusz Dziekanowski scores four of Celtic's five goals as they beat Partizan Belgrade 5-4 in the UEFA Cup but still go out on away goals after the tie finishes 6-6 on aggregate. 1990 John Collins becomes Celtic's first £1million player when he signs from Hibernian. 1991 Billy McNeill is dismissed as Celtic manager after two successive trophy-less years.

Brian McClair and Maurice Johnston, the highly successful striking partnership of the mid-1980s, energetically challenge Hamish McAlpine, the Dundee United goalkeeper.

—LEGENDS—

Danny McGrain

Full-back play at Celtic took on new dimensions once Danny McGrain had made the right-back spot his own at the club. That position would remain almost exclusively in his possession for the 17 years after his debut in 1970 and throughout that time Danny excelled – not only was he a teak-hard defender with an uncanny ability to tackle with precision and power, rarely losing out to an opponent, but he was without parallel as an overlapping defender with the pace, creativity and imagination to assist the attack. During the 1970s he was among the finest full-backs in world football.

Danny's sterling qualities as a footballer would have been noteworthy in themselves but what made him even more exceptional was the degree of adversity that he overcame during his career. Shortly after establishing himself in the team, in 1972, he suffered a fractured skull; after appearing for Scotland at the 1974 World Cup he was diagnosed diabetic; and in 1977 he suffered an ankle injury that forced him to miss the World Cup in Argentina and that kept him out of the game for 18 months. It says much about his character that Danny's style and exuberance were not diminished in the least by any of those setbacks.

Laraine McGrain, Danny's wife, jokingly threatens to shave off his beard prior to Celtic's trip to play Partizani Tirana of Albania in the European Cup in September 1979. Enver Hoxha, the Albanian leader, had banned the cultivation of beards but Danny was given special dispensation to wear the beard for Celtic's trip to the then politically isolated country.

> " *He made things so easy for you if you were playing in front of him.*
>
> Bobby Lennox "

Danny, dependable as ever, provides sterling back-up for Davie Provan (left) after Dom Sullivan has tackled Billy Abercromby in a match with St Mirren in 1981.

RIGHT: A moment of fun for Danny while representing Scotland at the 1974 World Cup, as a West German policeman displays that famous German sense of humour in larking around with Danny and Jim Stewart, the goalkeeper.

ABOVE: Tommy Burns, Dom Sullivan and Davie Provan take up the Spanish theme by wearing sombreros in advance of the European Cup quarter-final with Real Madrid in 1980. Johnny Doyle takes it all a bit further by opting for the full bullfighter's outfit.

LEFT: Davie Provan and Johnny Doyle having fun at the hairdresser's as they each undertake the necessary preparations for having a perm.

ABOVE: Roy Aitken and Tommy Burns, two of the most influential players for Celtic during the 1980s, pound their way through training in the first summer of that decade. Roddie MacDonald follows them over the hurdles, under the demanding exhortations of Frank Connor, the coach.

LEFT: The *Daily Record* reports on Celtic's last-gasp victory over Rangers in May 1979. Having been 2-1 down and playing with only 10 men following Johnny Doyle's dismissal, Celtic came back to win 4-2, Murdo MacLeod's fierce 20-yard shot in the final seconds capping the drama and bringing Billy McNeill rushing off the Celtic bench in jubilation.

143

Frank McGarvey, accompanied by Murdo MacLeod, races off in delight after scoring the first goal in what would be a 6-0 victory over Diosgyoeri Miskolc of Hungary in a 1980 European Cup Winners' Cup tie.

You'll have to stop cheating like this… The pace and threat that Davie Provan possessed for Celtic is reflected in the damage done to his strip by desperate opponents slowing him down illegally by trying to take the shirt off his back.

ABOVE: More blatant means appear to have been used here to stop Davie Provan as the Celtic winger clutches his face following an encounter with Willie Johnston, the Heart of Midlothian outside-left.

LEFT: Some respite for Davie Provan as he receives what looks like a slightly unorthodox method of treatment for the stresses and strains suffered on the field of play from Brian Scott, the Celtic physiotherapist, with Murdo MacLeod awaiting his turn.

147

148

A Riotous Affair

It took police on horseback to disperse the Celtic and Rangers supporters who had begun fighting each other on the pitch after the 1980 Scottish Cup final. Police who had been on duty at the match had been re-deployed outside after the final whistle to deal with fans in the streets outside the stadium, but that left only a skimpy police presence to deal with the supporters who were left behind inside the ground. The longest-lasting and most important outcome of the riot was the Criminal Justice (Scotland) Act 1980, which banned alcohol from Scottish football grounds.

Middle Men

Bob Valentine, the referee, bravely steps in between Davie Provan and Willie Johnston as the two wingers go toe to toe in an Old Firm derby.

ABOVE: Don McVicar, the referee, appears to be in a slightly impatient mood as he addresses Murdo MacLeod in a match with Hibernian.

RIGHT: Jim Duncan, the referee, intervenes following the altercation between Frank McAvennie and Chris Woods, the Rangers goalkeeper, in the 2-2 Old Firm draw at Ibrox in October 1987. McAvennie and Woods were dismissed by the referee and those two players, along with Graham Roberts, on the left, and Terry Butcher, the Rangers captain, were subsequently charged with disorderly conduct and breach of the peace. All duly appeared in court, where Butcher and Woods were found guilty, the charges against Roberts were not proven and McAvennie was found to be not guilty.

151

Young Guns

Billy McNeill with a quartet of budding young talents in 1982, from left, David Moyes, Danny Crainie, Paul McStay and Charlie Nicholas. The club was still capable of producing good young players and Nicholas, the striker, was the brightest star at the club in the early 1980s. McStay would excel as a stylish midfield player and would be central to every Celtic team over a 15-year period. Moyes was a more modest footballer, being allowed to leave Celtic for Cambridge United in 1983, but he found his métier in management, most notably with Everton. Crainie scored the opening goal seconds into his first Old Firm derby at the age of 19 in April 1982 but he too would leave Celtic in 1983, for Wolverhampton Wanderers, although he returned to Celtic Park as a youth-team coach in the mid-1990s.

ABOVE: A stork-like Charlie Nicholas moves the ball away from David Hayes, the
Morton captain, during a match in the spring of 1983. Nicholas, who did his best to
live up to a "Champagne Charlie" image as a high-living footballer, would be still
only 21 when transferred to Arsenal in the summer of 1983, against the advice of Billy
McNeill, who felt the player ought to remain at Celtic and mature further before going
to England. The striker, though, had suffered a broken leg 18 months previously, a
reminder of the insecurities of football, and when the London club offered him wages
five times those available at Celtic Park, the offer was too tempting for him to resist. His
play for Celtic in the 1982-3 season, when he notched 48 goals in all competitions, had
been simply exquisite and he was never to recapture that style in his subsequent career
with Arsenal, Aberdeen and at Celtic again in the first half of the 1990s.

153

Murdo MacLeod, watched by Paul McStay, scores Celtic's fourth goal in the spectacular 5-0 defeat of Sporting of Lisbon in the UEFA Cup in November 1983. The player, who moved on to Borussia Dortmund in 1987, suggests that this was the finest Celtic performance during his nine years at the club.

Sponsorship of football and of football teams became ever more predominant during the 1980s, with bigger money available from firms who saw that with the game being shown more frequently on television, and often live, there was the opportunity to advertise to a large and captive audience. Here, in a match at Ibrox, John McClelland, the Rangers centre-back, tries in vain to dispossess Davie Provan, the Celtic winger, with Rangers' historical Archibald Leitch-designed Stand looking less distinctive than usual thanks to its criss-cross balcony feature being used as a hoarding for an extra advertising banner almost in the way someone might drape untidily a wet beach towel over the balcony of a holiday apartment block.

The 1984-5 season saw Celtic for the first time following the practice of having a sponsor's name on their shirts. The first sponsor was CR Smith, a local double-glazing firm, who simultaneously agreed to sponsor Rangers' shirts as it was believed that sponsoring one half of the Old Firm and not the other would lead to an adverse business reaction. Here the Celtic team prepares for the 1985-6 season with the sponsor's logo emblazoned on their jerseys. Some Celtic supporters have never become used to this distortion of the famous Hoops, and the way in which one of the most distinguished shirts in world football has been defaced. A club whose directors proclaim it to be special might do well to eradicate shirt sponsorship entirely or follow the example of Barcelona, who really have shown themselves to be different by either keeping the jersey entirely free of a shirt sponsor or donating the available chest space to a charity such as Unicef.

An Unhappy Occasion

When Rapid Vienna arrived in Glasgow for the second leg of their European Cup Winners' Cup tie with Celtic in November 1984, the Austrians were in confident mood. Not only did they have a very strong and talented team but they were 3-1 up from the first leg. A goal in Glasgow would have put the tie almost beyond Celtic's reach but instead the Viennese were overwhelmed by the excellence of Celtic's play on the night and the backing they received from a packed and exuberant Celtic Park.

When Celtic, 3-0 ahead, were awarded a penalty, the Rapid players protested long and hard to Christer Drottz, the Swedish linesman stationed in front of the "Jungle" terracing, and Kjell Johanssen, the referee. Both stood firm so Rudi Weinhofer, the Rapid player, fell to the ground clutching his head, claiming he had been struck by a missile from the crowd. UEFA bought it and ordered Celtic to replay the match 200 miles from Glasgow, an encounter they lost 1-0. Drottz, years later, said of Weinhofer, "He was pretending. When Rapid appealed and UEFA decided to replay the game, that was the wrong decision." That did little to help Celtic in 1984, though. They had been robbed of a place in the quarter-finals that they believed was rightfully theirs, in a competition they had thought they could win. Instead, they had to look on as Rapid went all the way to the final, where they lost to Everton.

LEFT: Amidst much confusion and a 15-minute delay to the match, Weinhofer is carried off the field.

BELOW LEFT: Hans Krankl, the Rapid captain, points to the touchline as he prepares to lead his players off the field in the match in Glasgow. Only the intervention of a Rapid official convinced Krankl not to follow this course of action.

BELOW: A Celtic supporter attacks Herbert Feurer, the Rapid Vienna goalkeeper, in the goal in front of the Stretford End at Old Trafford during the replayed second leg. Another Celtic supporter would, at the conclusion of the match, run on to the field and attack Peter Pacult, the striker, who had scored the only goal of the game. As punishment for these assaults on Rapid players, Celtic were forced to play their next European tie, a Cup Winners' Cup match with Atletico Madrid in 1985, behind closed doors.

RIGHT: The unique sight of a near-deserted Celtic Park for an elite match as Celtic take on Atletico Madrid in the European Cup Winners' Cup in October 1985. After a credible 1-1 draw in Spain, Celtic lost this second leg 2-1 and those who participated believe that the lack of a home crowd affected Celtic much more than Atletico.

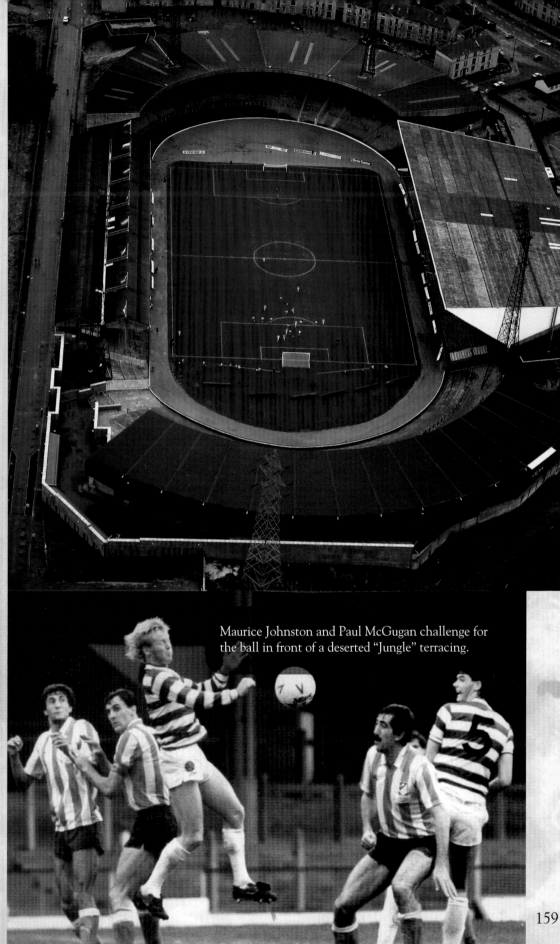

Maurice Johnston and Paul McGugan challenge for the ball in front of a deserted "Jungle" terracing.

The arrival of Graeme Souness as Rangers manager in April 1986 added a new dimension to the traditional Old Firm rivalry. Until that point, Celtic and Rangers had paid their players more poorly than clubs at the top level in England and, in pooling the best Scottish talent, had relied on players' loyalty to make up for the sizeable difference in the rewards they were missing through remaining at home. Souness increased the stakes by paying players in the fashion to which they were accustomed in England and was thus able to draw to Ibrox a number of high-profile English players, with continental internationals later to follow.

Celtic would be forced to keep pace with this radical change in Scottish football. Until that point in the 1980s, their closest and most regular rivals for trophies had been not Rangers but Aberdeen and Dundee United. Now the focus was firmly back on Glasgow and the renewed impetus given to the club across the city who had not won a League title since 1978.

ABOVE: Peter Grant sends his shot past Chris Woods, the England international goalkeeper, in the 2-2 draw at Ibrox in October 1987. Following his goal on this highly charged occasion, Grant skidded on his knees in the direction of the Celtic support, all the while making the sign of the cross.

RIGHT: Representatives of the two clubs would still be friendly away from the action as here, with Graham Roberts, one of Rangers' newly recruited England internationals, posing for a fun picture with Andy Cameron, the comedian, and Roy Aitken.

160

ABOVE & LEFT: On the field, the newcomers added an edge to the Glasgow derby, with English players such as Terry Butcher absorbing themselves to the full in the great rivalry between the two Glasgow clubs and taking it just as seriously, if not more so, than the locals. Here Mark McGhee and Roy Aitken appear unsuccessful in offering a handshake to Graham Roberts at the end of the derby of August 1987, which Celtic had won 1-0 through a silky Billy Stark goal and in which Graeme Souness had been dismissed for a wild lunge at Stark.

Marking the Centenary

Pierce O'Leary, Roy Aitken and Tommy Burns snap away to get the first pictures of four of the new recruits to Celtic who did much to provide the impetus to make the 1987-8 centenary season memorable. The new players are (clockwise from top left): Billy Stark, Mick McCarthy, Andy Walker and Chris Morris.

Peter Grant makes a driving run through midfield during the centenary season, with John Collins of Hibernian almost matching him for determination. Celtic were unstoppable that season, losing only three games from 44 in the League as they won the title and they would go on to clinch the Scottish Cup by defeating Dundee United 2-1 in the final, with Frank McAvennie scoring the winner in the final seconds of the match.

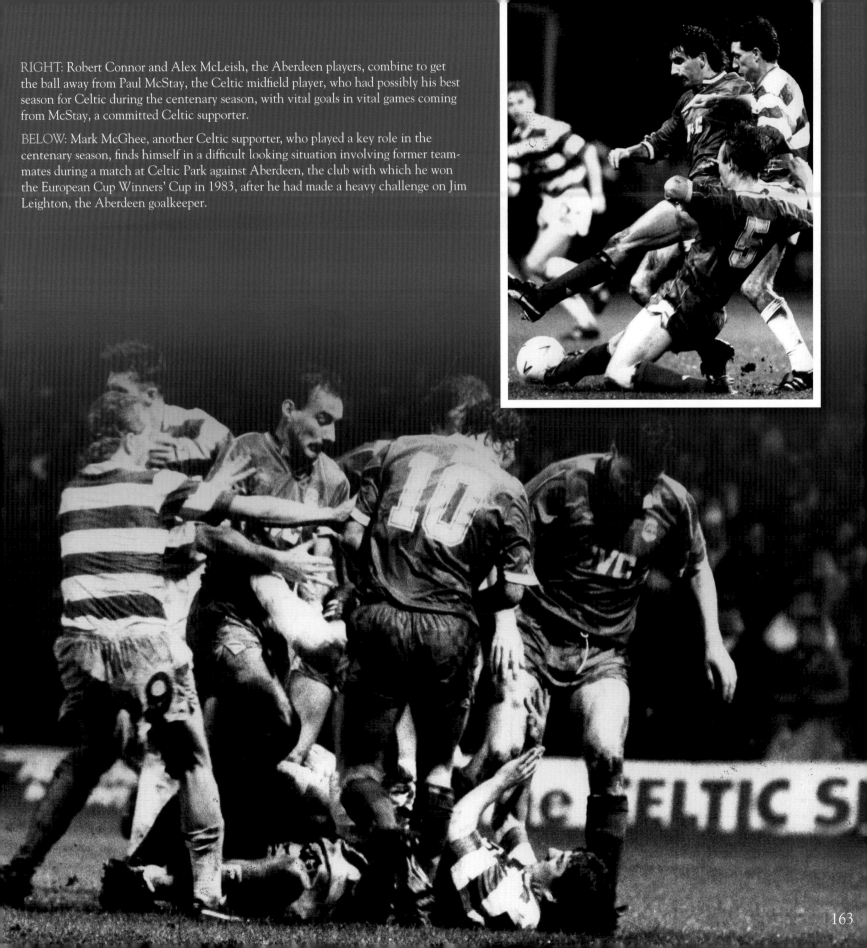

RIGHT: Robert Connor and Alex McLeish, the Aberdeen players, combine to get the ball away from Paul McStay, the Celtic midfield player, who had possibly his best season for Celtic during the centenary season, with vital goals in vital games coming from McStay, a committed Celtic supporter.

BELOW: Mark McGhee, another Celtic supporter, who played a key role in the centenary season, finds himself in a difficult looking situation involving former team-mates during a match at Celtic Park against Aberdeen, the club with which he won the European Cup Winners' Cup in 1983, after he had made a heavy challenge on Jim Leighton, the Aberdeen goalkeeper.

163

Margaret Thatcher, the prime minister, was at Hampden Park in May 1988 to present the Scottish Cup to the winning team in the Scottish Cup final, which, on the day, proved to be Celtic. Anton Rogan follows Billy Stark in holding up the trophy.

LEFT: The presence of Margaret Thatcher as guest of honour at the 1988 final was not universally popular with the Celtic supporters.

ABOVE: Tommy Burns shows how much winning the centenary double means to him.

Beating Hearts

Frank McAvennie's goals helped Celtic win the League and Cup double in their centenary season but the striker, after playing just 50 games for Celtic, returned to West Ham United in March 1989. Here he takes a tumble in a match with Heart of Midlothian in December 1988, which Celtic won 4-2.

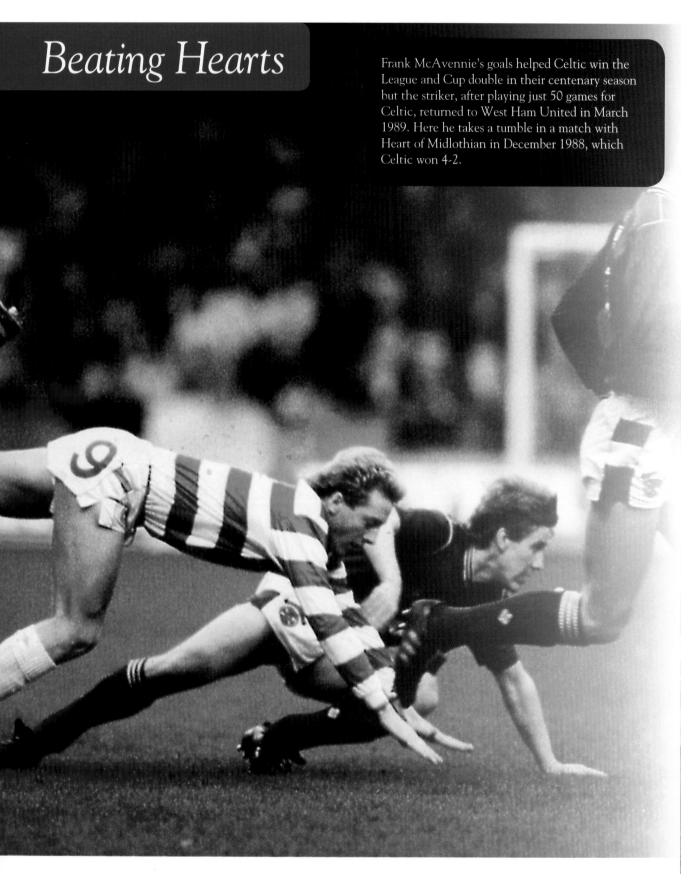

LEFT: Roy Aitken leads a posse of Celtic players determined to dole out retribution to Tosh McKinlay, the Heart of Midlothian player, during a fiery encounter between the clubs in March 1989.

BELOW: Tommy Coyne would be a leading goalscorer for Celtic in the lean years of the early 1990s. Here he makes his debut in the 1-0 victory over Heart of Midlothian at Tynecastle in 1989 after signing from Dundee.

A packed Celtic Park played host in 1989 to Liverpool in a match of remembrance for the victims of the Hillsborough Disaster. It was Liverpool's first outing since the tragedy.

Jagged Peaks

When Partizan Belgrade arrived at Celtic Park for the second leg of a European Cup Winners' Cup tie in September 1989, they were 2-1 ahead from the first leg. The events that followed, and which were witnessed by 50,000 inside Celtic Park, were quite extraordinary. The Yugoslavs took an ominous-looking lead after only seven minutes but Dariusz Dziekanowski, Celtic's newly-signed Polish international striker, equalized to make the score 1-1 at half-time. Celtic went ahead, again through Dziekanowski, after the interval, but Partizan equalized to make it 2-2. Once more Dziekanowski put Celtic ahead and again Partizan equalized, to make it 3-3. Goals from Andy Walker and Dziekanowski put Celtic 5-3 up but with only two minutes remaining, and Celtic still pushing for nothing less than a sixth goal, Sladjan Scepovic scored for Partizan to make it 6-6 on aggregate, sending Celtic out on the away goals rule.

It was one of the most extraordinary performances in Celtic's history for Dziekanowski to score four times against a highly skilled Partizan team but all the good work had been undone by Celtic rushing to look for more goals and leaving themselves open defensively as the game reached its conclusion. "I felt we climbed three mountains in 90 minutes and then threw ourselves off of them," Billy McNeill, the Celtic manager, said. Still, Dziekanowski's performance offered grounds for optimism. Again, these were to be quashed. The man from repressive, communist Poland would, as McNeill put it ruefully later, enjoy the freedoms of the West a bit too much and, with his off-field activities draining him of his strength, the Polish playboy's football suffered and he would never again reach such heights with Celtic before being ushered out of the door to Bristol City at the beginning of 1992.

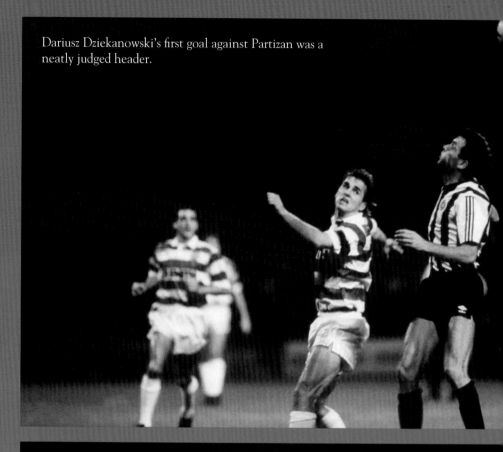

Dariusz Dziekanowski's first goal against Partizan was a neatly judged header.

The Pole scores Celtic's second goal.

Dariusz Dziekanowski celebrates his second goal in the process of becoming the first Celtic player to score four times in a single European match.

"
To be involved in a game like that was just amazing but after a performance such as that we should have gone through.

Paul McStay
"

Goran Pandurovic, the Partizan Belgrade goalkeeper, for once gets the better of the man nicknamed "Jacki" by the Celtic supporters.

Dariusz Dziekanowski, in a match with Hibernian, displays the athleticism and style that made him such a potentially exciting player for Celtic.

ABOVE: Dariusz Wdowczyk, his fellow Pole, who arrived shortly after Dziekanowski, proved a more durable signing.

Things have to be going badly for Billy McNeill, the great enthusiast for all things Celtic, to be feeling the edge of despair, as here in the dugout at Celtic Park in December 1990 with his team slithering through a second successive trophy-less season. McNeill felt undermined by sometimes vicious internal politics and unsupported by the board of directors of the time in his efforts to keep abreast of a Rangers side that was strengthening constantly with high-profile signings.

Billy McNeill leaves Celtic Park in 1991 after having been dismissed as manager, cheered on his way by all varieties of enthusiasts.

—LEGENDS—

Paul McStay

Paul McStay was Celtic's most consistently excellent performer of the 1980s and 1990s. His calm creativity and imaginative use of the ball was evident from the moment he made his debut as a 17-year-old in 1982 until he was forced to retire by a serious ankle injury in 1997. His role in the team was to use his refined skills to prompt good things out of others but in the 1987-8 centenary season, when everyone at Celtic felt a deep need to win the League to commemorate the founding of the club, McStay was just as driven as more rugged performers such as Roy Aitken and Peter Grant.

Those who were surprised by McStay's gritty attitude as Celtic won that League and Cup double underestimated the determination that lay below the surface of this amenable and generally reserved man. A subtle player, McStay's positioning, movement and intelligence were fully appreciated by his team-mates, especially when times became tougher for Celtic as the vibrant 1980s ended and the more difficult 1990s got under way.

Paul McStay takes the ball away from John Robertson, the Heart of Midlothian player.

> *He would see things, score goals, support people. He made passing seem easy.*
>
> Danny McGrain on Paul McStay

Nicely poised and balanced, Paul McStay confronts Partizan Belgrade challenges during the 1989 European Cup Winners' Cup tie.

FOOTBALL
-STATS-

Paul McStay

Name: Paul Michael Lyons McStay

Born: 1964

Playing Career: 1982–1997

Clubs: Celtic

Celtic Appearances: 677

Goals: 72

Scotland Appearances: 76

Goals: 9

Paul McStay gets a lift in training from Murdo MacLeod and Davie Provan.

A New Lease of Life
1992-1998

" *This is the club for me.*

Henrik Larsson on Celtic

"

Simon Donnelly scores Celtic's first goal in the enthralling 6-3 UEFA Cup victory over SC Tirol Innsbruck of Austria in 1997.

1992 Tony Cascarino, Celtic's record £1.1million signing, leaves the club for Chelsea only six months after joining. 1993 Liam Brady resigns as Celtic manager after having failed to win a trophy since being appointed to that position in 1991. 1994 Fergus McCann leads the successful takeover of Celtic and begins an ambitious plan to redevelop Celtic Park. Tommy Burns succeeds Lou Macari as manager, with Macari dismissed after only nine months in the job. First division Raith Rovers inflict a devastating defeat on Celtic by winning the League Cup final on a penalty shootout. 1995 Celtic defeat Airdrieonians 1-0 in the Scottish Cup final to win their first trophy for six years. Rod Stewart opens the new 26,000-seater North Stand. Paris Saint-Germain inflict a record home defeat in European competition on Celtic by winning 3-0 in the second leg of their European Cup Winners' Cup tie. 1996 Celtic lose just one League game in 36 but draw 11 and finish second to Rangers in the Premier Division. 1997 Tommy Burns is replaced as manager by Wim Jansen, the former Holland international, who quickly moves to sign Henrik Larsson from Feyenoord. Jansen leads Celtic to a League Cup victory with a 3-0 defeat of Dundee United in the final. 1998 Henrik Larsson finishes his first season at Celtic as the club's leading goalscorer with a total of 19 goals. Jansen leads Celtic to their first championship victory for 10 years and then resigns two days later.

The Lisbon Lions applaud as Lady Jean Stein opens the Jock Stein Stand in August 1998; the third new stand to be completed at Celtic Park in three years.

Time for Change

The opening half of the 1990s saw a fierce battle of wills develop at Celtic Park as supporters began to clamour for the removal of the individuals who comprised the board of directors at the club. The directors responded by becoming even more entrenched in their determination to hold on to power. The supporters' demands for change were based on the directors' lack of impetus in attracting investment to the club and creating an infrastructure that would enable Celtic to challenge Rangers, who were by then dominating Scottish football with the financial backing of multimillionaire David Murray.

ABOVE: Supporters agitate for the resignations of Kevin Kelly, the chairman, and his fellow directors.

RIGHT: The pressure on the directors becomes more visceral: during an Old Firm match in January 1994 coins and pie foils are thrown in their direction during the match. Celtic capitulate to lose 4-2, sending Rangers on their way to a sixth successive League title.

The Celtic directors attempted to rebuff their detractors by insisting that they had plans in place to construct a spanking new stadium on a vacant site in Cambuslang that would also play host to assorted revenue-generating businesses for the club. An architect's plan for the new stadium and the supposed launch of the enterprise were put in place in April 1992 when Kevin Kelly visited the site of the new ground, along with Gwynn Kennedy, the chairman of the Superstadia group, to promote the grandiose idea through the press. When it finally became clear, in February 1994, that the board had been unable to raise the funding for the venture, the failure hastened their demise as Celtic directors.

McCann's the Man

Fergus McCann, third from right, the tough Scots-Canadian entrepreneur, shortly after spearheading the dramatic March 1994 takeover of Celtic to begin its transformation into a more dynamic, business-minded enterprise. His financial nous would enable the club to construct a 60,000 all-seater stadium, and when he left Celtic in 1999 a club that had been lurching towards bankruptcy in 1994 was on a sound financial footing.

RIGHT: Upon Fergus McCann's departure, in early 1999, some of the supporters, at least, were determined to display gratitude for his efforts on the club's behalf and the effects of his drive and determination.

BELOW: Some of Fergus McCann's radical ideas, such as his "Bhoys Against Bigotry" campaign, to fight sectarianism, did not go down too well with some of his own supporters, and during his five years as managing director of the club he was often accused of parsimony because of his determination to run the club prudently.

Celtic were forced to spend the 1994-5 season using Hampden Park as their temporary home ground while the three terraces at Celtic Park were razed to the ground to prepare for reconstruction of the stadium. Here Tony Mowbray, the centre-back, scores in the 2-1 victory over Dundee United in August 1994, the first home League match that season.

Cup Contrasts

Paul McStay turns away in despair after missing his penalty-kick, Celtic's sixth in the shootout with Raith Rovers in the 1994 League Cup final. The match, against the first division side, had been viewed by many Celtic supporters as the ideal opportunity to capture a trophy again after a five-year barren spell, but Rovers played with conviction and commitment to secure a 2-2 draw after extra-time and held their nerve well in the shootout to deal a hammer blow to Tommy Burns' team.

The Scottish Cup proved to be a happier
competition for Tommy Burns in the 1994-5 season,
with Celtic defeating Airdrieonians 1-0 in the final
in May. Here Burns, with the Cup still bedecked
in green and white ribbons, enlists the help of Rod
Stewart, singer and Celtic fan, to show it off at a
charity match held for the Davie Cooper appeal, in
honour of the Rangers and Scotland winger, who
had passed away after suffering a brain haemorrhage
at the age of 39 in March 1995.

Andreas Thom became the first player on whom Celtic had spent more than £2million when he joined from Bayer Leverkusen in the summer of 1995. Celtic had never previously signed a player of his pedigree – Thom had 61 caps for East Germany and Germany combined – but he showed only occasional flashes of brilliance for Celtic during his three years at the club.

A Visit to the Black Sea

Celtic's qualification for the European Cup Winners' Cup in 1995 offered the club the chance to test itself in European competition for the first time since Fergus McCann had engineered the takeover and Tommy Burns had become manager. The draw paired them with Dinamo Batumi of Georgia and demonstrated the type of interest and variety that European football can offer.

Georgia was in political turmoil. Armed gangs roamed the streets and Celtic expressed concern about the security of their players and supporters. The Georgians duly laid on 5,000 security police to monitor the 18,000 crowd at the first leg, which Celtic won 3-2.

ABOVE RIGHT: One of the Batumi players has a difference of opinion with Peter Grant.

RIGHT: Andreas Thom scores the opening goal in Celtic's 3-2 win in Batumi.

There is an almost rural feel to the Tsentral Stadium as Rudi Vata, Celtic's Albanian defender, walks off the park with Andy Walker, the striker, and John Hughes, the centre-back, leading the way, after the first-leg victory in Georgia, which would be complemented by a 4-0 win in the second leg at Celtic Park.

Pierre van Hooijdonk, the striker signed from NAC Breda of Holland in January 1995, and the scorer of Celtic's sole goal in the 1995 Scottish Cup final, pursues Stephane Mahé, the Paris Saint-Germain full-back, in the European Cup Winners' Cup tie at Celtic Park in 1995, which would conclude in a 3-0 win for the French side. Mahé would later join Celtic, in the summer of 1997.

The sparky rivalry between Celtic and Rangers continued to engage all comers during the 1990s as the largely English imports of the 1980s were joined by an influx of foreign players, some of whom, in temperament, were made for such occasions.

Paolo Di Canio, signed by Celtic from Milan in 1996, confronts Ian Ferguson, the aggressive Rangers midfield player, at the conclusion of an Old Firm derby in 1997 by using his hands to mimic a snapping gesture, as if of a limb being broken; especially sinister when coming from someone from the land of Mafiosi. Ferguson clearly took exception to it all.

> *You could take all the derby matches in the world, add them all together and they still wouldn't equal one-millionth of the Old Firm. There is nothing like it.*
>
> Paolo Di Canio

Jackie McNamara, the Celtic full-back, gets up close and personal with Mark Hateley, the assertive Rangers striker, as Enrico Annoni attempts to intervene.

John Rowbotham, the referee, intervenes to restore order as a Celtic–Rangers meeting in September 1995 blows up. Almost the entire Celtic team are milling around in the vicinity of Richard Gough and Ally McCoist, the Rangers players. The Celts are, from left, Andreas Thom, Pierre van Hooijdonk, John Hughes, John Collins, Paul McStay, Phil O'Donnell, Gordon Marshall, Tosh McKinlay, Simon Donnelly and Rudi Vata.

Fan Power

Celtic supporters outside Celtic Park give vent to their anger at Tommy Burns being relieved of his duties as Celtic manager in May 1997. After the early 1990s, when active fan protests had helped rid the club of an unpopular board of directors, Celtic supporters felt ever more confident and potentially powerful in voicing protest.

Back on Top

The appointment of Wim Jansen in 1997 gave Celtic their first foreign manager or, as Fergus McCann had decided to re-title the position, head coach. Following Tommy Burns' three years as Celtic manager, during which there had been a great deal of friction between manager and managing director, McCann was determined to restructure the football set-up at Celtic. Jansen would report to Celtic's first director of football, Jock Brown, who until then had been best known as a football commentator, although he also specialized in sports law and negotiation at a legal practice in Glasgow.

New frictions soon arose between Jansen and Brown. "My relationship with Jock Brown was bad from the beginning to the end," Jansen would say, but Celtic still won the League title that season to end Rangers' dominance of Scottish football and simultaneously prevent the Ibrox side breaking Celtic's record of winning nine successive League titles. Despite all that, Jansen opted to walk away from the job at the end of the season, thus becoming the only Celtic manager to have left the club at the end of a League title-winning season.

Marc Rieper, a Danish international centre-back signed from West Ham United in 1997, was a vital component in Wim Jansen's title-winning team. Here he prepares for training in November 1997 with a pensive-looking Andreas Thom, who would feature only sporadically under Jansen. It would prove to be the German's final season at Celtic.

ABOVE: Marc Rieper
and Craig Burley get into
the retro kit to publicize
the opening of the Celtic
museum in November 1997.

LEFT: Wim Jansen takes the
Celtic players through his
final training session as head
coach, in Lisbon, Portugal,
two days after securing the
League title for the club.
It was in the Portuguese
capital, prior to a friendly
match with Sporting,
that Jansen called a press
conference to announce
that he would be quitting.

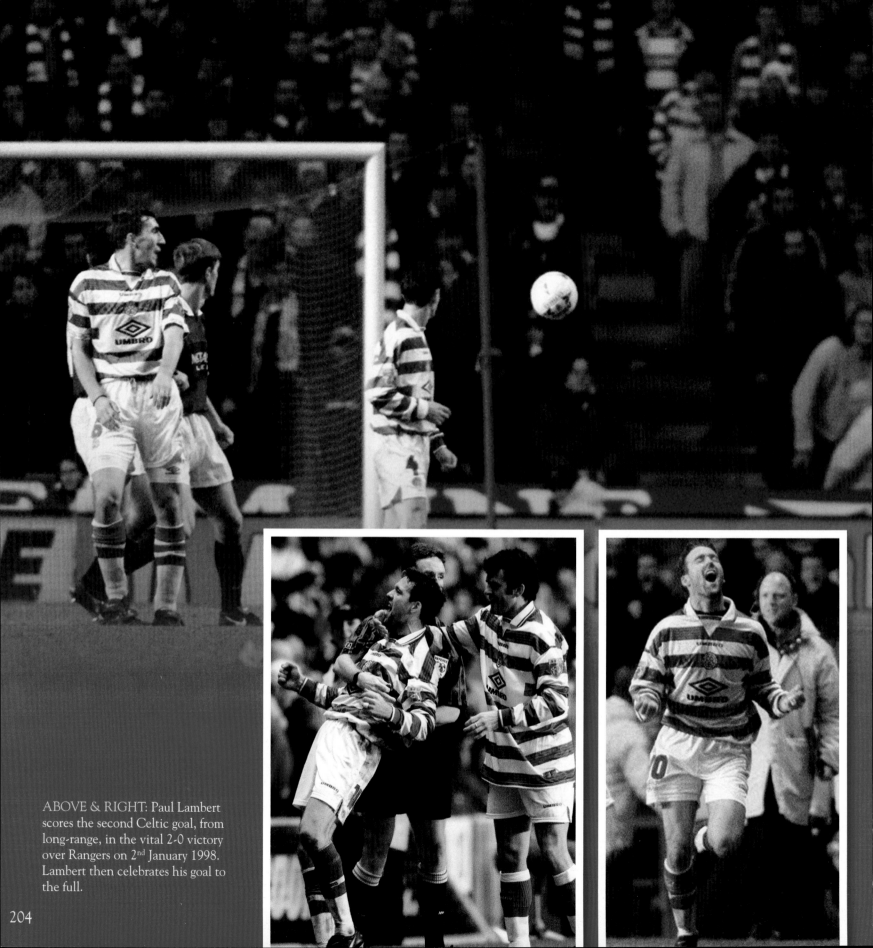

ABOVE & RIGHT: Paul Lambert scores the second Celtic goal, from long-range, in the vital 2-0 victory over Rangers on 2nd January 1998. Lambert then celebrates his goal to the full.

RIGHT: Simon Donnelly, Celtic's young poster boy of the late 1990s, in the spotlight for a fashion shoot in the summer of 1998.

–LEGENDS–

Henrik Larsson

Wonderful goals, carved out with the precision of a master craftsman, made Henrik Larsson an almost mythical figure at Celtic even while he was still playing for the club. At a time when footballers were just starting to earn more and more ridiculous sums of money, with almost every passing year, and when sticking with one club consequently became deeply unfashionable, Henrik rewarded Celtic for giving him a platform to develop his skills by remaining true to the club throughout the prime years of his career.

As well as his penchant for putting the ball in the net with style, a skill he shared with Kenny Dalglish, one of his predecessors at Celtic, he equally delighted in working assiduously for his team-mates and creating chances for them. A self-motivated individual, and hugely brave inside the penalty area, where the tackling and the challenges are at their sharpest, Larsson scored a wide variety of goals: thumping headers, precise free-kicks, chipped shots on the run and snappy, quick-reaction, close-range finishes. Henrik Larsson was the nearest thing to a flawless footballer that Celtic have ever had.

The warm welcome that Henrik received from the day he signed for Celtic in 1997 helped ensure that he would reciprocate fully.

"*This is where I made myself as a player and I am eternally grateful to Celtic for giving me that opportunity when other clubs didn't want to know me.*"

Henrik Larsson on Celtic

FOOTBALL
–STATS–

Henrik Larsson

Name: Henrik Edward Larsson

Born: 1971

Playing Career: 1988–2009

Clubs: Hogaborg, Helsingborg, Feyenoord, Celtic, Barcelona, Helsingborg, Manchester United (on loan)

Celtic Appearances: 315

Goals: 242

Sweden Appearances: 106

Goals: 37

The 19 goals that Henrik Larsson scored during his debut 1997-8 season for Celtic made him the top scorer for that season and did much to tilt the title Celtic's way.

The author would like to thank:
Richard Havers for his help and support during the creation of this book; Paul Moreton for the chance to put this book together; Brian Gallagher for invaluable, friendly advice and for digging out so many excellent pictures; Ann Marie Nimmo at the *Daily Record* for patiently collating and sending pictures; Kevin Gardner at BrainWave; and Dave Scripps at the *Daily Mirror*

Special thanks to Billy McNeill